"NO OTHER AMERICAN PRESIDENT WAS MORE LOVED AND MORE HATED. NONE WAS MORE SKILLFUL A POLITICIAN, YET SO DISPARAGED BY THE INTELLECTUAL FIGURES OF HIS TIME. NONE WAS SO PATRICIAN, YET ABLE TO WIN THE HEARTS OF THE POOR AND UNEDUCATED. NONE GUIDED THE NATION THROUGH SO MANY UP-HEAVALS AS FRANKLIN DELANO ROOSEVELT. AND NONE TODAY STANDS OUT SO SHARPLY AS THE MODEL OF WHAT AN AMERICAN LEADER SHOULD BE."

—*Los Angeles Times Book Review*

"Lively . . . apt . . . Alsop has an insider's natural grasp of the family, its background, its secrets . . . Franklin Roosevelt shaped our nation in this century: he gave Americans hope and enacted social programs that, in Mr. Alsop's words, 'included the excluded.' Such precious gifts are worth remembering, with all the love and respect that an author can muster."

—*The New York Times*

"Alsop combines the perceptions gained as a distant Roosevelt relative with the gifts that have made him one of our most distinguished political journalists for more than four decades . . . a grand birthday present honoring Roosevelt's memory—a knowing, witty and consistently interesting portrait of a leader who was 'singularly longheaded, singularly patient, singularly realistic, and singularly bold.' "

—*Chicago Tribune Book World*

". . . a sensitive ⟨. . .⟩ rib-ute to FDR's co⟨. . .⟩ not blink at his sho⟨. . .⟩ of photographs giv⟨. . .⟩ er-sonal memoir."

⟨. . .⟩*obe*

A CENTENARY REMEMBRANCE

FDR

1882-1945

BY

JOSEPH ALSOP

includes selections from
picture sections compiled and written by Roland Gelatt
photo research by Laurie Platt Winfrey

WASHINGTON SQUARE PRESS
PUBLISHED BY POCKET BOOKS NEW YORK

A Washington Square Press Publication of
POCKET BOOKS, a Simon & Schuster division of
GULF & WESTERN CORPORATION
1230 Avenue of the Americas, New York, N.Y. 10020

Published by arrangement with The Viking Press
Library of Congress Catalog Card Number: 81-68381

ISBN: 0-671-45891-4

First Washington Square Press printing November, 1982

Originally published in Great Britain by Thames and Hudson Limited

10 9 8 7 6 5 4 3 2 1

CONTENTS

INTRODUCTION

Thus far—and I cross my fingers—the United States has been a remarkably fortunate country, and the lucky Americans, with their wide lands, their vast resources, and their happy place between two sheltering oceans, have been much envied. Yet the most unlikely aspect of American luck has hardly been noticed abroad or at home. On the rare occasions when the nation has encountered real danger, a great leader has always come forward in the time of need to see the United States through its peril. Franklin Delano Roosevelt is one of the proofs of this surprising rule.

The year 1982 is the centennial of Roosevelt's birth; and it is also the fiftieth anniversary of his first election in 1932. Americans have seen no less than eight Presidents take the oath of office since Roosevelt's death at Warm Springs, Georgia, in 1945; and he is already a remote and half-legendary figure. Yet few today will deny that he was one of the great Presidents in the classic American mold. Even on the very short list of great Presidents of the first order, furthermore, Roosevelt has a special distinction. Just as George Washington was needed twice, to lead the American Revolution and then to take the lead in founding a new government on a more secure foundation, so Franklin Roosevelt had to deal with the devastating danger of the great Depression and then to deal with all the dangers of the Second World War until he died on the eve of victory. He too was needed twice, and twice he met the need.

When he died, he had been in the public spotlight more or less continuously for three and a half decades; and he had lived and worked in the full glare of the White House for over twelve years. Yet to this day, Roosevelt's central achievements remain incompletely understood. And despite the exploration of huge archives and the publication of many thoughtful studies, Roosevelt the man also remains more than a little mysterious.

From afar, he was always charming, always impressive, always more than life-size; but at close hand, he could too easily seem artificially genial, less than forthright, and more than a little superficial. At his death, a nation wept and so did half the world; but in life he was hated with passionate near-unanimity by Americans of his own kind. More important, he was appraised with varying degrees of condescension, often extreme and frquently hostile, by a high percentage of the leading intellects of his time.

Most important of all, even those who were closest to him during his years in the White House, in fact the very men whose names he made large in the land, often regarded him primarily as an inexhaustible source of energy and power—an invaluable source because the power was so vast, a worrying source because too easily misguided, and thus a source always in need of being guided and manipulated, of being *aimed* like a fire hose, so to say, in order to get done what really needed doing.

Yet these men who so often thought they were using the President, which means most of the first group of New Dealers, many of the second group, and even a good many of those who staffed the war effort, never fully understood their real situations and their relationships to their chief. Consciously or instinctively, Roosevelt was deftly using them while they thought to use him. When they ceased to be useful to him, they were also discarded as casually as morning papers sufficiently skimmed. By the same token, the Cabinet officers and high advisers whom he positively encouraged to fight out their policy differences with bellicose publicity always tended to suppose that the President was a man incapable of choosing between right (their side of the argument) and wrong (the other side). While they openly belabored one another with everything short of baseball bats, these eminent public servants in fact never seemed to suspect what was really happening.

Meanwhile, the President was wickedly amused by the spectacle of his subordinates' squabbles. He was anything but averse to his resulting role of fatherly arbiter. And he benefited greatly (and nothing pleased him more than making an unobserved gain) by the chance to test the trends of public and Congressional opinion, and thus to see exactly how far he could comfortably go himself. Nor did he care in the least that this way of carrying on the government appeared shockingly disorderly to solemn editorial writers, to foreign observers of every kind, and to all sorts of other persons who never learned the two main rules for judging what Franklin Roosevelt was up to—that this President used others but was never used himself, and that he cared greatly about results and rather little about how the results were obtained.

For these and many other reasons, the second Roosevelt was certainly the most enigmatic (or so it seems to me) of all the major Presidents so fortunately produced by the United States. Yet certain aspects of Franklin Roosevelt, both as man and man of action, were the opposite of enigmatic, and may therefore be offered as fixed points, or dependable bearings, for anyone who seeks to assess his leadership. This is worth doing, too, for he will soon belong to history alone. The time is not far off, in fact, when no one will still be here who was old enough at the time to retain a vivid memory of the Roosevelt Presidency.

As a man of action, to begin with, he was singularly longheaded, singularly patient, singularly realistic, and singularly bold. How his plans and aims invisibly matured, seemingly like organic growths in the back of his mind, and how his strange sense of timing really worked, are subjects worthy of long special study. No American leader has ever operated in quite so unexpected a way or possessed a comparable sense of timing. The fixed points here are that he almost never failed to wait until the right moment to do what he wanted to do, and that when the moment came he repeatedly did what others did not dare to do because it seemed too difficult, or too costly, or too defiant of all the old known rules of American political behavior.

As for Roosevelt the man, he was certainly no plaster saint. In certain ways he could obviously be thoughtless, even unfeeling. He and his wife, for instance, married when both were painfully young and inexperienced. She had had a downright ghastly childhood and youth; and he had had an immensely happy childhood and a youth altogether comfortable and if anything overprotected. It was up to him, if it was up to anyone, to help her reach some sort of accommodation with married life and with her peculiar new surroundings.

Instead, if one may judge by the whole volumes to be read between the lines of Mrs. Roosevelt's revealing, decep-

9

tively innocent-appearing autobiography, he seems to have been content to live on the surface of their common life, as it were, thereby causing Mrs. Roosevelt to retreat over and over again into what she herself later condemned as "Patient Griseldaism." He expected her, in fact, to be what she was never likely to be, the cheerful, conventional wife of a prosperous young New Yorker belonging to the special group they both came from. He was patient with her. He apparently put up without protest with long fits of silent but ostentatious wifely martyrdom that would have driven most men to the madhouse or the divorce court. Yet was this not, perhaps, because he did not care very much whether his wife felt martyred or not? At any rate, he did nothing to ease her way or to protect her. Above all, he left her wholly unprotected against the relentlessly domineering ways of his possessive mother.

Nowadays such a marriage would be likely to break up within a year or so. Instead, it endured until he died, finally worn out by the constant toil and fearful burdens of his great office, and in the arms of another woman only a few minutes before he drew his last breath. Yet almost no persons who bulked large in his life were so useful to him as Mrs. Roosevelt, nor was she the only human being from whom he took much without much thought about the taking.

None can doubt, however, that Franklin Roosevelt was a truly good man. Here the tests are simple: which sides he chose at every turning in his remarkable career. He was against, indeed he was the unrelenting enemy of misery, poverty, oppression, cruelty, injustice, meanness, smallness, obscurantism, and every other form of nastiness and source of unhappiness that human beings and their societies are given to, and he was the stout friend of plenty, generosity, decency, liberality, geniality, openness, justice, and freedom. In truth, he loved the light and loathed the darkness, and in hard and testing times he was also inspired and sustained—a point no longer fashionable to make but a true point none the less—by a simple, rather old-fashioned, but deep and unshakable Christian faith. No one not wholly warped by one of the mindless ideologies of left or right can remember the condition of the United States in 1932, or the danger to the world in 1939, without concluding that Franklin Roosevelt belongs on the very short list of very great Presidents.

What, then, were his most important achievements? In

10

world affairs, his central achievement nowadays seems obviously enough, but it is generally forgotten now that what he achieved seemed utterly impossible at the time. From the foundation of the government under George Washington until close to the end of Franklin Roosevelt's second administration, the situation of the United States was always essentially the one described in Bismarck's envious joke, which I used to hear in the paraphrase of the late Justice Felix Frankfurter. In the Frankfurter version (for which he took entire credit), the joke was: "God Almighty takes care of infants, drunkards, and the United States of America." What the joke meant, of course, was that unlike everyone else in this harsh world, Americans had no need to take much thought or to watch their steps with care because they had a whole rich continent to exploit and develop without any discernible external risk or threat to worry about.

But the point is that when most Americans unquestioningly believed their wholly unique national situation was not only normal but eternal, and thus required no effort to protect it, President Roosevelt quickly saw that the foundations were being undermined and had to be protected. God Almighty could no longer be safely relied upon to take care of the country Roosevelt led, because of new forces let loose upon the unhappy world in Roosevelt's time. Politically, the new forces were best typified by Adolf Hitler, but there was also the less obvious new force of technological change. This process of change has now gone much further; but even in the 1930s the whole world was already shrinking in a way that spelled ultimate doom for the former American continental isolation. In the circumstances, the essential thing to do was to persuade the nation to shoulder the responsibilities of an active great power directly involved in the changing world's affairs and future. Doing just this was Franklin Roosevelt's magnificent and unforgettable feat in the field of foreign policy.

Compared to the feat itself, this detail or that of wartime policy, even the President's sometimes naive dealings with Joseph Stalin, all sink into total unimportance. For good or ill, the role of the United States in the world today is owed to Roosevelt, or rather to his wisdom and courage in facing up to the wholly novel challenges confronting him, and to the way he contrived to meet those challenges against amazingly heavy odds.

As to his central achievement on the home front, it seems

11

to me still more magnificent, yet even today it is not well understood. This is because I do not believe that the real essence of Roosevelt's achievement on the home front is to be found in the list of new federal agencies he founded, or in the new balance of power between the business community and the government which he sought and obtained, or even in the inauguration of the American version of the welfare state, for which he was responsible. Instead, the essence of his achievement, at least that part of his achievement which gave the whole true grandeur, derived in differing degrees and in hardly perceptible ways from the combined impact of all his domestic reforms. On a very wide front and in the truest possible sense, Franklin Delano Roosevelt included the excluded.

This will now seem an unlikely claim to most people at home and abroad, because of the vocal and wholly proper American preoccupation in the last twenty years with the part of the job still remaining to be done—particularly the inclusion of the still partly excluded black Americans. What has been accomplished already has therefore been almost ignored. Yet it was a very great accomplishment, historically unparalleled as far as I know in any other nation-state of the modern world; and this huge first part of the job was mainly the work of Roosevelt.

It is not easy to grasp how enormous the contrast is between the United States of today and the United States whose leadership Roosevelt assumed in a time of deep trouble after the 1932 election. The truth is that the America Roosevelt was born into in 1882, and the America I was born into in 1910, and even the America of 1932, was an entirely White Anglo-Saxon Protestant nation by any practical test.

This does not mean the nation did not contain a huge minority recruited from other stocks and strains. The largest part of the minority was Catholic, being composed of the Irish, the Italians, the French Canadians, the Poles, and all the other groups the politicians now call "the ethnics." Next in order of numerical importance came the millions of blacks in the South, then the Jewish Americans, the Spanish speakers (then mostly in the Southwest), and finally all sorts of groups of more exotic origins, including the small groups of Japanese Americans and Chinese Americans, who suffered far harsher exclusion than the black Americans at that time. Yet the presence within the borders, among the work force, and even on the citizenship-rolls of so many people of other origins did not in any real way alter the fact that America in 1932 was still a WASP country in all significant respects.

The nation's history, as then known by citizens of all possible origins, was WASP history. The nation's culture was a WASP culture. The nation's economy was WASP-dominated, with only a small percentage controlled by Jewish Americans and others (who frequently took on WASP protective coloration as soon as they could boast of a certain material success). Even the nation's politics were WASP politics, with no more than the big cities controlled by the Irish, and only the big cities in the North at that, and mainly in the Northeast, too.

There were a great many poor White Anglo-Saxon Protestants, of course, but it was still true—even obtrusively true—that WASPs owned while almost everyone else rented, WASPs hired while others took jobs, and WASPs made loans while others borrowed. Even at Harvard College, a *numerus clausus* of 10 percent was still imposed on Jewish applicants for admission. For that matter, as late as 1955 John F. Kennedy was rejected the first time he was nominated for the Board of Overseers, because the majority of the voting alumni of Harvard were even then not ready to see as Overseer this Irish Catholic who became an Overseer two years later and would be elected President of the United States only five years later. In almost all the major universities, too, only the utmost proven eminence in a scholar's chosen discipline could overcome a lack of WASP coloration when major appointments were under consideration.

It is hard to credit, and few remember, that these conditions and restrictions still continued in full force when Roosevelt was inaugurated at the climax of the great Depression, with close to a third of the work force unemployed and the banks shut and seemingly bankrupt. It is not easy, either, to pinpoint precisely how everything was transformed during Franklin Roosevelt's terms in office. Yet there can be no doubt that he wrought the transformation by direct and indirect means; and there can be no doubt, either, that he was furiously blamed for it. This was the real reason rich Americans "went to hiss Roosevelt" at newsreel theaters, because they truly hated him. This is why he was called "a traitor to his class." The vast majority of the really rich Americans in those days belonged, in one way or another, to one of the regional WASP in-groups; in varying degrees the positions of many depended on continuing the old WASP exclusive dominance; and Roosevelt's threat to this dominance, rather than this Rooseveltian measure or that, was what produced the Roosevelt-haters.

In honesty, it should be said that there have been later minuses among pluses, in the usual way. Like a lizard dropping its tail, the United States has now lost both its former history and its old culture because both were too purely WASP. One may be sure that Roosevelt himself would have deplored both losses, not least because no coherent new American culture and no coherent new view of the American historical identity have as yet replaced what was lost.

Yet only consider. At the time of Franklin Delano Roosevelt's inauguration close to 50 percent of all Americans were in some degree excluded from the full rights enjoyed by all WASP Americans (except for those few living in ancient, isolated pockets of primitivism and poverty, like the Appalachian mountain people). More particularly, non-WASP Americans, however able, were excluded from the normal opportunities of any moderately fortunate WASP. In some cases, the exclusion was downright shocking, as with the blacks and the Americans of Asian origin. But in all cases the exclusion was there, whether in greater or lesser measure, and it was felt and bitterly resented. To Roosevelt, therefore, about 40 per cent of all Americans now owe the fact that they have become undoubted "citizens with a full share" (to borrow a phrase from General De Gaulle). This gigantic achievement further prepared the way for the long effort, still happily in progress, to give a full share to those who none the less remain partly excluded. "He gave tens of millions their full and rightful share at last" seems to me an honorable epitaph, and although Franklin Delano Roosevelt did not finish the job, it is a true epitaph for him.

Such, then, is the best I can offer as an introduction to this centennial essay on Roosevelt's life, career, and total contribution. Perhaps, however, I should add a few words about my own credentials for attempting such an appraisal. To begin with, I have some special knowledge, since I belonged to an outlying branch of the same extensive tribe. My grandmother, Mrs. Douglas Robinson, was Theodore Roosevelt's younger sister; Eleanor Roosevelt's father was TR's younger brother; and my mother and Mrs. Roosevelt were therefore first cousins as well as dear friends from childhood. In addition, my mother, like Eleanor Roosevelt, was a distant cousin of the second President Roosevelt.

Then, too, my grandmother was a close friend of the President's mother, Mrs. James [Sara Delano] Roosevelt, and of the President's much older half-brother, James Roosevelt Roosevelt, and his second wife, Betty. Finally, my mother's brother, Theodore Douglas Robinson, married Helen Roosevelt, the daughter of this older half-brother of the future President, and my uncle was also a Harvard friend of Franklin Roosevelt, although this friendship was later disrupted by politics.

Given this bizarre web of interrelationships, an anthropologist's approach to kinship terms was needed, for instance, to work out the links between the Franklin Roosevelts and their children on one side, and the children of my uncle, Theodore Douglas Robinson, on the other. The Robinson girls were "half-great nieces" of the President and "half-first cousins once removed" of his children, both through their mother, the President's half-niece. I spare the reader the further kinship terms needed to define the relationships of the young Robinsons and Roosevelts because their fathers were remote cousins, and the equally complex ones required by the fact that Theodore Douglas Robinson and Eleanor Roosevelt were also first cousins. It is enough to say that in the kind of tribe I came from, all these relationships and their degrees of closeness were known and measured. It all seems very long ago, rather like Tahiti before Captain Cook.

As for myself, we Alsops were not so deeply entangled in the web. Yet in the way that was then usual, the young Alsops were brought up to call Mrs. James Roosevelt "Cousin Sally," Mrs. Franklin Roosevelt "Cousin Eleanor," and so on through the older generation, although of course the President, once elected, instantly became "Mr. President." Many of the Cousins This and That were also familiar figures of my childhood and youth; for most of the senior members of the tribe lived in large "family houses," as these redoubts were called—three are now museums—and there was a good deal of visiting back and forth. But I shall call all tribal persons mentioned hereafter by their public rather than their tribal names.

In any case, these tribal links are only worth recalling for two reasons. In the America of those days, if you were brought up in fairly close branches of the same tribe, you knew the tribal atmosphere and circumstances reasonably well and so could judge the situations and actions of persons

15

in the other branch, and you also learned all the accumulated tribal lore about the members of the other branch. In addition, largely for tribal reasons, the President's wife, the President himself, and the President's mother all offered me occasional hospitality and showed me much kindness during my early years as a political reporter in Washington; and besides giving me well remembered pleasure, this gave me, as a minor but acknowledged member of the tribe, a chance to see them all intermittently in a way that was not usual.

Still more important for my assessment of President Roosevelt, however, was my extra-tribal experience, first as a reporter and then in the war. I began work on graduating from Harvard in 1932 in the New York newsroom of the old *New York Herald Tribune*. At the end of 1935 the *Herald Tribune* sent me to Washington, where my first assignment was covering the U.S. Senate. Washington was still not far from a village in those days, and before long I knew the village well and had done well enough myself to be offered an opening as a political columnist—a job with a lot more leverage then than it has now. The late Robert E. Kintner and I started our column together in 1937, when I was barely twenty-seven. By the end of another year "Alsop and Kintner," as the feature was usually called, had again done well enough to make us both what may be defined as very minor but heard voices. It was this, in turn (if I am to be honest with myself), which permitted me to forge links on terms of near equality with the more important men who came to Washington when "Dr. Win the War replaced Dr. New Deal"—as the President described the transition.

With some of these, to be sure, like Dean G. Acheson and James V. Forrestal, I had old-fashioned WASPish personal connections. Barring the most senior ones like Henry L. Stimson, however, I made friends with them all, including Harry L. Hopkins—or so I like to think—before I went off to the War in the Far East in 1941. As long as each man lasted, moreover, these friendships continued, and some, I am pleased to say, continue to this day. Here, however, they are only relevant because of the exceptional chances they gave me to see something through more knowing eyes of President Roosevelt as Commander in Chief in the making, and then after I left Washington in the spring of 1941, as Commander in Chief in war.

In sum, I was fortunate enough to have a whole series of opportunities as an observer of Roosevelt that were not given to many other Americans of my age. The fruits of these observations, plus the tribal lore I remember, plus what has been added by the large volume of subsequent writing about Roosevelt, plus the results of my own ruminations on the past in turn add up to what has been set down here.

COUNTRY GENTLEMAN

The first step to take in any attempt to understand and assess Franklin Delano Roosevelt is to try to understand the situation and ambience he was born into. At this very first point of departure, moreover, a high proportion of recent students of Roosevelt have tended to go wrong; for they are sadly given to describing him as an "American aristocrat." There is no such thing, and anyone using that phrase would have been dismissed as "common" at Hyde Park or any other house inhabited by members of the tribe Roosevelt belonged to. Nor is that all. I can remember being taught as a very young man by an older female mentor of the tribe that it was even "common" for American officials to use or to be called by courtesy titles, such as "Hon." for a Congressman or Cabinet member, "because you must remember, darling, Mr. Adams's titles of honor bill was wisely rejected by the first Congress."

Later, I got into trouble in Washington by foolishly following this ancient rule. I must add, however, that I still think it the right rule, and I still cringe when I hear, for example, a seedy political appointee to an Embassy abroad being breathlessly addressed, even mentioned by his own wife, as "Ambassador This" or "Ambassador That." All too often, "Mister" would be excessive. But that is by the way.

Before the changes of mental habit that politics impose, Franklin Roosevelt, his wife, and his mother were likely to have called the families of the sort they came from "nice people," or in moments of extreme shock or angry reproof of

17

the young, "ladies and gentlemen." I myself used to call them the "who was shes," from the all but universal feminine response when a married couple known only by the husband's name was somehow mentioned. "Now, let me see, who was *she?*" the women would always say, gazing contemplatively at the ceiling; and one of those present would almost always come up with a name and an identifying tag, such as "She was an X, but one of the poor ones from Albany, you know," or perhaps "Y, but one of the lunatic Y's from Providence, of course."

The domain of the "who was shes" was the Northeastern United States, with a few rather special extensions beyond the Alleghenies and an outpost in San Francisco. All else belonged to the unknown in the first decades of the 20th century, although this curious recognition system had extended deep into the older South before the Civil War. The chief citadels of the "who was shes" were New York and Boston; and both the future President and his wife bore one of the more recognizable New York names. In his case, the name carried the added tag, "the Hyde Park lot, you know," and in hers, "Oyster Bay, of course."

Both were in fact born into places in old New York which are best described in a passage in that invaluable guidebook to the past, Edith Wharton's *The Age of Innocence:* "The New York of Newland Archer's day [the early 1870s] was a small and slippery pyramid in which, as yet, hardly a fissure or a foothold had been made or gained. At its base was a firm foundation of what Mrs. Archer called 'plain people'; an honorable but obscure minority of respectable families . . . who had been raised above their level by marriage with one of the ruling clans . . . Firmly narrowing upward from this wealthy but inconspicuous substratum" were the somewhat less numerous "ruling clans" already referred to, and even these were not the "apex of the pyramid." In the period Edith Wharton was writing about, this apex was still composed of a rather tightly knit bloc of the very oldest New York families—Stuyvesants, Beekmans, Rutherfurds, Jays, Livingstons, Van Rensselaers, and one or two more. These were often exceedingly rich by the standards of those days, most frequently because they had acquired and hung on to huge areas of real estate, sometimes in the 17th century, and in any case when land was still selling at close to Indian prices.

It should be added that by the time of Franklin

Roosevelt's birth in 1882, all sorts of fissures and footholds in Edith Wharton's slippery pyramid were just beginning to appear. For one thing, there would soon be a set which was called "the swells" in the newspapers of that day. Among "the swells," the men played polo and rode hard to hounds. The women were usually beautiful, and at a minimum did not follow the old New York practice of "summering and wintering" their dresses from Worth before they wore them. (Again, see Edith Wharton.) The practice of adultery was also widely suspected, correctly in a few cases. Although non-adulterous, Mrs. Roosevelt's father and mother belonged to this set before alcoholism overcame Elliott Roosevelt.

Even more significantly, moreover, fissures and footholds were also appearing in the pyramid under the pressure of the tremendous influx of new money. In Edith Wharton's terms, the apex of the pyramid in Roosevelt's youth and manhood had thus become an amalgam of the vastest new fortunes and toughest and most admired old families. One more short passage may also be borrowed from *The Age of Innocence:* "'Don't tell me,' Mrs. Archer would say . . . , 'all this modern newspaper rubbish about a New York aristocracy . . . Our grandfathers and great-grandfathers were just respectable English or Dutch merchants, who came to the colonies to make a fortune and stayed because they did so.'"

That was exactly the history of the Roosevelt family, whose Dutch founder came to the United States in the 17th century. The wealth of the Hyde Park branch then began with the fortune made by the founder's grandson Isaac, who had a highly successful sugar refinery in the back yard of his New York house in the early 18th century. As for the Roosevelt place in Edith Wharton's pyramid, it is best described as middling; and the place of the Hyde Park Roosevelts might well have been even less than middling by the later 19th century. Money always mattered; and the future President's father, James Roosevelt, was an ambitious but bad businessman, while his grandfather, another Isaac Roosevelt, had wholly abandoned business for a country life at Hyde Park. But these Roosevelts, like so many old New Yorkers, had the habit of marrying well.

Isaac's wife had brought with her a handsome share of the large Aspinwall fortune. The first Mrs. James Roosevelt was one of the rich Howlands, and the second, the future

President's mother, also had a large fortune from her father, Warren Delano. And the President's much older half-brother took as his first wife one of the daughters of Mrs. Astor, the formidable lady who set out to rule the New York world of her era, and largely succeeded because the Astors were the only older New York family with a quantity of money huge enough to be fully competitive with the new money. James Roosevelt Roosevelt was also the only one of the family to play any real role in what used to be called the "world of fashion." The President's older half-brother even kept a four-in-hand for a while, a major gesture; but I only recall him in old age, as a sweet and immensely kindly elderly man who lived quietly in retirement at Hyde Park with his enchanting English second wife.

All this may seem singularly unimportant, but the point is that both Franklin and Eleanor Roosevelt *thought* differently when they were young. She recorded that as a young married woman she still believed what she had been taught, that "New York Society was important"; and she further indicated that one of her husband's bitterest early disappointments was his failure to be elected to his preferred undergraduate club at Harvard—to be specific, the oldest of these clubs, the Porcellian, to which James Roosevelt and Theodore Roosevelt had both belonged. It should be added, finally, that Franklin and Eleanor Roosevelt even began by attaching a certain importance to the distinctly silly trappings affected in the later 19th century by the upper group of old New Yorkers. Family crests had been claimed, usually falsely, by the richer American families. This began, particularly along the Eastern seaboard, in the early 18th century or even before that. But in the later 19th century, the crests began to be insisted upon (on writing paper, for instance), perhaps to put down those with new money, and family liveries for menservants were added in some places, above all in New York.

Mrs. Roosevelt's bridesmaids at the wedding all had to wear three Prince of Wales feathers nodding on their heads because this unbecoming ornament was the (surely invented) Roosevelt crest, and the ushers were given Prince of Wales feathers stickpins. As for the family livery, the last Roosevelt to have people in livery in his own establishment was pretty certainly the President's half-brother, for the grooms are in livery in a photograph of James Roosevelt Roosevelt's four-in-hand; and while his Astor wife was alive

d he had a New York house, the footmen no doubt wore
very. Although there were never liveries in the main house
Hyde Park, the family livery was also the theme of one of
e entertaining exercises in sweet malice that were Eleanor
oosevelt's special mode of humor—and extremely funny
e could be in this quiet way, always pretending total inno-
nce, even though she wholly lacked any sense of the ri-
culous.

This story, as was rather often true with these exercises,
as at the President's expense, and concerned their first
ys in the White House in 1933. At that time the White
ouse male staff was composed of ushers (white) and but-
rs and doormen (black). The doormen had somewhat sur-
isingly been put into livery a little after Theodore
oosevelt restored the White House to its early and beauti-
l state. Apparently by chance, moreover, they were pro-
ded with Roosevelt livery, or something very like it. These
stumes then survived, without recorded protest from the
oormen; but long before the 1932 election, Mrs. Roosevelt
d come to detest anything with the least taint of
orldliness and fashion. Hence, she wished to put the White
ouse doormen into more normal dress instantly.

"Unluckily," she would add with a little laugh and the
ecial intonation used for such purposes, "Franklin noticed
at it was *Roosevelt* livery." In reality, he too had lost any
ace of the old snobberies by 1932. He merely liked unex-
ected reminders of his tribal past and his own past, which
as why he insisted that dangerously incendiary real candles
ould continue to be lit on family Christmas trees, because
at was how it had always been done. But still, the White
ouse doormen kept their livery until after the Second
orld War, when Harry S Truman abolished the practice.

All the foregoing may well seem trivial and eerily remote
day. The "who was shes" of the past had a surprisingly
ong run for their money, from the 17th century until the
reat Depression of the 20th century; but in the main, they
ave become the nobodies of today. The first point to note,
owever, is that they were not nobodies during most of
ranklin Roosevelt's lifetime. Instead, the richer and more
rofessionally successful invariably belonged to the leading
roup in whatever city or town they inhabited, and they
uite often dominated these groups. They retained great
verage in the business community of the Northeastern
nited States, which was then the predominating source of

finance of much of the rest of American business. They provided most of the members of the governing boards of most of the more important universities, charitable institutions, and other establishments controlled by boards of trustees, at least throughout the Northeast. Above all, until after the First World War, they were what is now called the role models for most other Americans, and by no means in the Northeast alone.

This was the corner of the past from which Franklin and Eleanor Roosevelt both came. It formed their manners, gave them their characteristic modes of speech and accents, inculcated their tastes (many of which the President always retained), and shaped their initial outlooks on their country and the world. Both eventually rebelled, albeit in varying degrees, against this past they came from, but if a personal past is powerful enough to promote rebellion, that in itself is a measure of its impact.

It should be added that, in different ways, the childhoods and younger years of Franklin and Eleanor Roosevelt were somewhat abnormal, as compared with the early years of other young New Yorkers of their kind and time. In the case of the future President, the abnormality—which was slight but still important, as I think—derived from the fact that he was brought up in a way that was already distinctly old-fashioned, perhaps because his aging father was distinctly old-fashioned. James Roosevelt was born in 1828, fought with Garibaldi (and was photographed picturesquely red-shirted) for a few weeks during a grand tour in 1848, went to Harvard Law School thereafter, and then went into business. Several of his business ventures were large in scope. For instance, he helped to organize the Consolidated Coal Company, which gained control of a large majority of the then-important Cumberland coal deposits, but the company ran into bad trouble in the wake of the panic of 1873. There were other ventures of the same sort, none of them successful, and in the main the elder Roosevelt busied himself with the management of small old family-connected companies like the Lake George Steamship Company. This did not keep him busy at all continuously, either; for most of each week he remained at Hyde Park, and his chief effort and time were given to his land and his herds there. He was in fact a country gentleman with a comfortable amount of inherited capital to support the gentlemanliness.

He had already settled into this pleasant, respectable, but fairly obscure niche when his Howland wife died in 1876. He was evidently one of those men who must be married, however, and four years later, although James Roosevelt was no less than fifty-two, he married the future President's twenty-six-year-old mother. It was an odd match, and it was at first opposed by the bride's father, Warren Delano, who owned another big Hudson River place, "Algonac," about twenty miles downriver from Hyde Park. Yet even the rich and masterful Delano could not find the match objectionable on any grounds except disparity of age; his daughter was determined to marry her elderly suitor; and so the wedding occurred in October 1880.

Her son's Presidency made Sara Delano Roosevelt in her old age into a national monument of sorts, but she only seemed to enjoy it in patches. She would have been less monumental if she had enjoyed it more, for one of her aspects as a monument was her refusal to relax by one particle the already fairly antique standards of proper behavior for ladies and gentlemen which she had early learned from her father. Thus she regarded many of the President's political associates and most of his advisers and staff as more or less unsuitable persons to receive at Hyde Park.

When the team of Benjamin V. Cohen and Thomas G. Corcoran were carrying all before them in the time of the second New Deal, she regarded them with deep suspicion. She even concluded she was being bilked because Tom Corcoran, while with the President at Hyde Park, was carelessly allowing his incessant telephone calls to be charged to her instead of to the U.S. Government. So she installed a pay telephone in the large front hall of her house, and forbade all outsiders the use of her own telephone. She could be unrelentingly stern, too, with politicians who seemed to her less than desirable guests, even if they were important for the future. Huey P. Long, for instance, wholly controlled Louisiana as long as he lived, and was therefore highly important. While still seeking to keep on good terms with Long, Franklin Roosevelt asked him to Hyde Park but avoided argument by giving his mother no warning. Seeing "the Kingfish" at her own table was too much for Mrs. James Roosevelt, and she retaliated. In a stentorian whisper audible to the entire table, she inquired blandly, "*Who is the awful man* sitting next to Franklin?"

In her young years, she had been a beautiful woman of the type that used to be called "queenly," and queenly she remained until she died in her eighties in 1940. She also retained her faculties unimpaired and her memory in excellent order. For example, her father had come close to losing his whole first fortune in the panic of the mid-1850s, and had therefore gone out to Hong Kong to rebuild his wealth as a partner in the principal American China trade house, Russell and Co. By 1862 he was doing exceptionally well, and although the Civil War was in full swing and Confederate commerce raiders were at sea, he sent for his wife and children. They came out by clipper ship around the Cape of Good Hope; and I can still remember hearing Mrs. James Roosevelt on the topic of this voyage on the Sunday before her son's triumphant 1936 reelection. She even sang, in a slightly cracked voice, the sea chanteys the clipper's sailors had sung making landfall at Java Head three-quarters of a century earlier.

In her childhood and girlhood, the life of the senior Mrs. Roosevelt had plainly centered on her father, which was perhaps why she chose to marry—and she had a wide choice—a man old enough to be her father. Once she was married, however, her entire life centered exclusively on her husband and then on her son. The result was a childhood and early boyhood for Franklin Roosevelt that was fairly unlike the early years of other young New Yorkers of his sort. The other families with big houses on the Hudson normally moved to New York for the winter and went to the country for weekends, which meant that the children early began to make friends of their own age at school and at such standardized reunions as the apparently eternal Mr. Dodsworth's dancing classes. (I myself remember being sent to Dodsworth's while staying in New York with my grandfather and grandmother at the age of seven or eight.)

It was quite different for Franklin Roosevelt, however. During a large part of the time, he was alone in the country with his father and mother, for they mainly remained at Hyde Park when they were not abroad, and he was again alone with his parents on the long pilgrimages to Europe the trio made every year. His father was affectionate and companionable; his mother was doting; his nurses and governesses were much attached to their handsome and lively charge; so he had a happy childhood and early boyhood. Nor

24

was he brought up in the least as a mollycoddle, for there were ponies and later horses to ride; there was the hair-raising winter sport, which his father loved, of ice-boating on the frozen Hudson; there was a whole big place to explore, and there were plenty of other things to do with enthusiasm that a true mama's boy would have avoided at all costs. But the fact remains that throughout his childhood and early boyhood, he was much more isolated from his contemporaries than had been the case with the great majority of the other boys he found at Groton, where he went, considerably later than was then usual, into the Third Form at the age of fourteen-plus.

I have emphasized this comparative isolation for a simple reason. I, too, was brought up in the country (in itself an odd formation for a prosperous young Northeasterner of the type likely to go to Groton) and I therefore went to Groton knowing only a single other boy there. It was a grim, even on occasion a desperate experience, and it took me over two years to learn to get on with my fellows and begin to make friends. Hence I suspect, perhaps wrongly and with only indirect evidence for my suspicion, that Franklin Roosevelt's much earlier experience was at least similar to mine and perhaps even worse.

It could have easily been worse, because the young male WASPs who went to Groton were even more stereotyped in the future President's generation than they were in mine. I was then too fat to be athletic, but he was too slender and a bit weedy as a youth, so neither of us had the supreme advantage (at Groton) of being good at games. But at least I was permitted to retreat into the library—although even in my time, a mother boasting of her son's precocious bookishness had been known to be told by Groton's famous Rector, Dr. Endicott Peabody, "Don't worry about it. We'll soon get *that* out of him." In Franklin Roosevelt's time, any taint of excessive bookishness was far more actively deplored, nor was general reading a refuge for him at any stage of his career, even though he had the invaluable knack of taking in and recalling the main points of a page of print with remarkable rapidity.

There is also indirect support for my suspicion that Roosevelt's Groton experience was somehow unhappy and may even have left scars. Eleanor Roosevelt herself shrewdly recorded that her husband had the feeling that so-

25

mething had gone sadly wrong with his time at Groton; and that he blamed his father and mother for sending him so belatedly. This, she said, was why he insisted on putting his own boys into the First Form in the hope that they would then make friends more easily than he had done because all would be new together, whereas Mrs. Roosevelt thought it was harsh to send them away at the age of only twelve.

What truly happened to Franklin Roosevelt when he went to Groton is worth taking time to consider, in turn, because of the peculiar atmosphere in which the future President was formed. Among his contemporaries of similar origins, whether male or female, being "popular" was then of almost inordinate importance—as so often in small closed groups. Popularity in turn derived from the correct mixture of personal qualities and personal advantages.

For men, good looks, being good at games, knowing the nuances of what Edith Wharton called good form and, perhaps above all, having a capacity for enjoyment and for communicating enjoyment, were on the whole the key qualities. In addition, it was an immense advantage to come from an admired family sufficiently well off to live handsomely if not ostentatiously—for the young of Roosevelt's New York and their equivalents in Boston and elsewhere were just as snobbish as their elders if not more so. Being intelligent, or at least obtrusively, ostentatiously intelligent was an actual drawback unless the intelligence was adequately counterbalanced by other, more dashing qualities—and young Roosevelt, although healthy, cheerful, and overserious, if anything, about the matter of organized sports, was somehow not at all dashing.

The fact is that, while never disliked, he never attained the grand goal of being popular, although he plainly wished to do so. This was just as much the case among the girls he danced with, when he was old enough to go to the big balls of that era, as it was among his male contemporaries. At least one historian has noted that the girls' name for him was "feather duster," because his brand of the badinage then thought suitable for female company was somehow unreal and unconvincing. My mother, who knew him well at that time, once told me that another feminine name for him was "the handkerchief box young man," because his good looks in those early years, though undeniable, too much resembled the rather awful good looks of the young men then customar-

26

ily portrayed on presentation boxes of feminine handkerchiefs.

There was also a solemn entry in an early diary which my mother made as soon as she learned of Franklin Roosevelt's engagement to Eleanor Roosevelt, to the effect that he was by no means good enough for her. It seems an unexpected observation in the light of hindsight, but it still has significance. So does the fact that Franklin Roosevelt had no greater success with his male contemporaries of the same sort—the real reason that he was not made a member of the Harvard club of his choice. This sort of thing would of course be wholly irrelevant, if it had not mattered to Roosevelt himself; but the evidence is unchallengeable that it mattered a lot to him. It gave him an "inferiority complex," according to his wife, and he once told a younger member of the tribe during the First World War that his worst disappointment as a young man was his non-election to the club his father and Theodore Roosevelt had belonged to at Harvard.

I would go further, too, for I believe it mattered a lot for his future. When he decided to enter politics in 1910, one factor was obviously his boredom with the law, and another was the example of Theodore Roosevelt, whom he vastly admired and plainly took as a model. But it seems to me all but certain that a third factor in his decision, perhaps subconscious, was the desire to stake out his own territory, where he would not be in competition with other young men of his own sort.

To this account of Roosevelt's boyhood and young years, only a couple of facts and one or two less tangible points need to be added. To begin with, Roosevelt had a good but far from brilliant academic record, mainly, one may guess, for the same reasons that at Harvard he gave his chief attention to "activities," such as editorship of the *Crimson* and, towards the end, the elections to class offices. Such activities, it may be noted, were then shunned like the plague by all the young men at Harvard who sought to be thought dashing. But what is of consequence is that, in youth and age, Roosevelt was never attracted to large intellectual subjects.

He was close to a speed reader, and he had a knack with the English language. But he was entirely without the wide-ranging interests and extensive knowledge of Theodore

27

Roosevelt, although he had detailed knowledge of subjects that particularly interested him, such as American history and the story of the American navy. Whereas Theodore Roosevelt was twenty-one when he published his first book, a quite serious essay on Admiral Mahan's theory of sea-power, Franklin Roosevelt, at very nearly that age, was writing distinctly embarrassing *Crimson* editorials about the Harvard football team's deficient fighting spirit. This limitation would matter later, when his world view began to matter greatly.

Few American leaders have known the United States, past and present, in quite the way Franklin Roosevelt did. For want of wide-ranging historical reading, however, his world view always retained something of the provincialism of the very provincial though very privileged American group he came from; and the results of this provincialism, especially when tinctured with Wilsonian idealism, could sometimes be unfortunate—although they had their good side as well.

As to the hard facts still missing, James Roosevelt, to whom his son was greatly attached, died of heart trouble while Franklin Roosevelt was at Harvard, whereupon his mother promptly moved to Boston to be near him. This astonishing move by Mrs. Roosevelt is interesting for two reasons. On the one hand, it reveals the possessiveness which was the senior Mrs. Roosevelt's dominant characteristic. On the other hand, it also reveals how far the President's mother was capable of carrying this possessiveness, precisely because the move was just as astonishing at that time as it would be today; and Mrs. Roosevelt was one who did not normally like moves, gestures, clothes, or anything else likely to raise eyebrows. It is no wonder, therefore, that when her twenty-two-year-old son told her that he was engaged to his distant cousin, Anna Eleanor Roosevelt, and wished to marry her forthwith, the senior Mrs. Roosevelt went to considerable lengths to prevent the marriage, including requiring Franklin Roosevelt to join her on a prolonged Caribbean cruise in the hope that he would forget all about it.

His mother had a weapon to use, too, because her husband had left her a considerable share of his fortune for her life and the place at Hyde Park as well, and she controlled her own large Delano dowry and inheritance. In all, therefore, his mother had about $1,300,000—substantial wealth in those days—as well as owning the house Franklin Roosevelt regarded as his real home to the end of his life. Meanwhile, he had only about $300,000 of his own, all told, as late as the middle 1920s when he invested heavily in the resort property at Warm Springs, where he still hoped to regain the power to walk. Until his mother's death, in fact, the largest part of his own unearned income must have been the allowance she paid him, in addition to providing a New York house for him. But although the senior Mrs. Roosevelt was entirely capable of using money as a weapon, she refrained from doing so in this case, and the marriage, with its bridesmaids and ushers all duly sporting Prince of Wales feathers, took place on 17 March 1905.

Probably Mrs. James Roosevelt gave way before her son's insistence on being married because she had no very good arguments to use against the match. Her prospective daughter-in-law, after all, was a wholly conventional choice for anyone in her son's position—if not exactly beautiful, at least well known for her goodness and seriousness, coming on both sides from families of just the right kind, and even possessed of what was then a pleasant though far from enormous income of her own from her mother's and father's estates. In the first years after the marriage, in fact, the wife's contribution to the joint resources was larger than the husband's.

Behind Eleanor Roosevelt's conventional facade as a well brought up New York girl, however, there lurked a personal history that was bound, in the end, either to produce a near-monster of worldly conformity or else—as happened—a most unconventional mature woman. Such a childhood and girlhood as she had somehow survived are all but unimaginable today.

Her father, Theodore Roosevelt's younger brother, was a man of great charm with an unidentified inner weakness—epilepsy was rumored, but it is unlikely. This had prevented Elliott Roosevelt from going to the university and further caused his early dependence on alcohol. He was an enchanting man, high spirited and amusing, a splendid horseman, a good companion, fond of the world, worldly in a way that was not common among the Roosevelts; but none of this could last long because of his ever-increasing alcoholism. His daughter Eleanor adored him. One can argue, in truth, that he was the great love of her life. But while she was a fairly small girl, he had to be shipped off to a huge stretch of land in the mountains on the Virginia-West Virginia border which Elliott Roosevelt's brother-in-law, Douglas Robinson, had inherited from one of his forebears. Besides being lumbered, the land was long used as a place to store family drunkards. These were numerous, and Eleanor Roosevelt had not a single close male relation of her own generation or the preceding one who did not end as a drunkard, with the sole exceptions of her President-uncle and her President-to-be husband. No wonder she loathed the very sight of any form of drink as long as she lived.

If anything, however, the beauty of Eleanor Roosevelt's mother must have been harder on her than her father's alcoholism. Mrs. Elliott Roosevelt was a rigidly conventional woman who somehow combined religious devotion and intense worldliness; but her most notable characteristic was her appearance, which caused her to be universally labeled "the second most beautiful woman in New York." "The most beautiful" was the ruling Mrs. Astor's daughter-in-law, Mrs. John Jacob Astor, who parted with her husband much later and then married Lord Ribblesdale. Physical beauty, one must add, was a quality taken exceedingly seriously in old New York.

With the elders attaching so much importance to good looks, it must have been extra hard on this gangling little girl with protruding teeth to have a famously beautiful mother. Her mother made no attempt to make it easier. She regularly called her daughter "Granny" because of her appearance. Once when my mother was having cambric tea with her cousin and friend, Mrs. Elliott Roosevelt actually turned to the two children and remarked, in a quite matter-of-fact tone, "Eleanor, I hardly know what's to happen to you. You're so plain that you really have nothing to do except *be good*." It was advice Eleanor Roosevelt followed all her life, but it cannot have been encouraging to hear at that age.

Far worse was to come, however. Mrs. Elliott Roosevelt died young in 1892, two years before her husband; and her mother's death left Eleanor Roosevelt mainly in the hands of her grandmother, Mrs. Valentine Hall. Mrs. Hall was both a beauty and the daughter of a Livingston. She owned a considerable share of one of the large Livingston properties along the Hudson, and here at Tivoli was the Hall house "Oak Bluffs." Her husband was also rich enough to keep a salaried house-theologian, so that he might indulge freely in his chosen pastime, theological inquiry. But Valentine Hall

30

died young without a will, and his wife, who had never even taken care of herself, then had to take care of herself, of the family property, and of the family too—above all, of her six strikingly beautiful children. Mrs. Hall received only a widow's share (with the rest of the money divided among the children, of course), and had never so much as signed a check. The results were predictable. She later developed a prudent tendency to say "No" to any proposals by her grandchildren, however reasonable. But she was putty in her own children's hands, and they controlled their own inheritances after they were of age.

One daughter, Mrs. Stanley Mortimer, married very well; and one, Mrs. Elliott Roosevelt, married what seemed well at first. But a third girl married Lawrence Waterbury, a handsome polo player and gambler without enough means to support either pursuit, and the fourth, "Pussie," had an endless succession of sentimental affairs which caused much talk. She further led the life of a beautiful and courted woman year after year without nearly enough money to pay for the innumerable smart turnouts which this then required, let alone the lady's maid essential to look after the turnouts. And she only married rather late in life, and again without enough money. (She was the chief model for Lily Bart, the unfortunate heroine of Edith Wharton's other best novel, *The House of Mirth*.)

As for the two Hall boys, Eddie married, while Vally did not, but what mattered above all was that both these handsome men became drunkards at an early age. Vally was in fact so bad that on one occasion when Eleanor Roosevelt was still hardly more than a child, one of his mad drunken fits inspired him to take pot shots at his niece in the garden at Tivoli from his bedroom window. In addition, all the younger Halls ran through their inherited fortunes at record speed except for Mrs. Mortimer and Mrs. Roosevelt; and as no one ever thought for one moment of taking a job, money was always desperately short for the effort they all put first on the list—the effort to keep up with the most glittering Joneses.

In this feckless atmosphere, distractedly presided over by an incompetent grandmother who had—I quote my mother again—"the greatest knack for making her surroundings gloomy of all the women in New York," Eleanor Roosevelt somehow got through her early teens, never for one moment forgetting her mother's injunction to be good.

Happily, she was then sent off to an English school run by a strong-minded and liberal Frenchwoman, Mlle. Souvestre, who had links with the Stracheys and other English intellectual families. She soon became Mlle. Souvestre's favorite. Not surprisingly, she loved the school, a major though incomplete liberation for her. But of course she had to come home in order to come out at the age of eighteen, because anything else was unthinkable.

Coming out cannot have been much fun, not least because she had to share a small New York house part of the time with her Aunt Pussie, still beautiful, still forever newly hopeful or newly heartbroken about one man or another, even more short of cash than ever, and habitually tardy to boot. To save on transport, they had to go out to their respective dinner engagements in the same conveyance; and Eleanor Roosevelt's autobiography relates a superficially pointless story of how the beautiful aunt's inability to be on time made the young niece so late for a big dinner at the Darius Ogden Mills's that the guests were already seated at table when she came in alone.

Only imagine a huge house smelling of money as strongly as of hothouse flowers; a hostess, Livingston-born like Eleanor Roosevelt's grandmother but still giving out no more warmth than a deep freeze decked with enormous diamonds (the largest in the city); an immense table of guests and a perfect throng of footmen—and all to be faced by a shy, still gangling, helplessly apologetic girl newly plunged into this larger, harder world. It must have been an agonizing moment, and since such moments cannot have been uncommon, one may guess that Eleanor Roosevelt was pleased to hear her Cousin Franklin's proposal and entirely willing to get married at the age of nineteen.

The other point to note is that as far as one can tell, the young couple had not yet rejected or even questioned any of the standards, conventions, values, or basic viewpoints taught them by their elders and accepted by their contemporaries of the New York of those days. Of their early life together, little needs to be said, except that they lived in a hotel until he passed his bar examinations; that the senior Mrs. Roosevelt then rented, furnished, and staffed a small house for them; and that they ended in the much larger house Mrs. James Roosevelt built for them, which they used until long after Franklin Roosevelt became President.

The tale of this last house needs to be told, for it is instructive though slightly out of chronological order here. To begin with, it was by no means an independent house, for it had been planned so that its main rooms could be thrown together with the main rooms of the adjacent house which Mrs. James Roosevelt had simultaneously built for herself. Communication between the two houses was therefore easy, and it proved to be much used over the years, not least by the future President's mother. Then too, both the senior Mrs. Roosevelt and her son had firm views about the design and decoration of the new houses, and rather than argue with them, Eleanor Roosevelt took refuge in a record fit of Patient Griseldaism. Thus she had had nothing whatever to do with any part or feature of her own new house, which was also expected to be her permanent New York base, until all was finished and she was proudly shown the results of her husband's and mother-in-law's efforts. A little while later, however, she was suddenly unable to maintain her Patient Griselda pose, and she fled into the adjacent house where she burst into floods of tears.

Incredibly enough, as she herself later recorded, when her husband learned of this, he had no inkling of what was wrong. He hurried to the scene, to be told that his wife did not like living in a house which was not her own in any possible sense; and he was still totally bewildered by both the outburst and her explanation. This suggests how little notice he had been taking of her earlier impersonations of Patient Griselda, and how much domineering by her mother-in-law Eleanor Roosevelt had previously accepted with no audible protest. Nor was this all.

As she later wrote herself, Eleanor Roosevelt made meek submissiveness to her mother-in-law a guiding rule of her early married life; and given her mother-in-law's character, there was a great deal for her to be submissive about. She was not a naturally maternal woman, either, and was often deeply worried about doing the wrong things with her children as they came along. The first was Anna. James, the first Franklin, Jr. (who soon died), and Elliott all followed in fairly rapid succession. The second Franklin, Jr. and John came a bit later. Yet the children were the opposite of an escape for their mother. Lacking any self-confidence in the nursery, she ended by handing them over to English nurses, to whom she also felt compelled to be submissive. Submissiveness in nurseries or elsewhere was not one of Mrs. James Roosevelt's traits, however, and it is not extreme to say that she all but stole her grandchildren from their cradles. The end result was an uncomfortable division of responsibility, with the mother in charge of instilling all the Dos and Don'ts which children have to learn, and the grandmother seeking to make pleasure-giving, sometimes verging on ruthless spoiling, into her special department.

Even Campobello, the Canadian island on the Bay of Fundy where the Roosevelts had long had a summer place, did not offer Eleanor Roosevelt enormous satisfaction. Mrs. James Roosevelt went there less and less often, while her son and his family fairly soon acquired a Campobello house of their own, and always spent Franklin Roosevelt's summer vacations there after one attempt to make a change. But at Campobello the children and their retinue had to be coped with as usual. Furthermore, Franklin Roosevelt had lost the weediness of his adolescence and first manhood, and was a fine horseman, an enthusiastic golfer, and a passionate sailor. His wife, for her part, loathed horses, had given up after one attempt to learn to play golf, and would not have enjoyed several days at sea, even if long coastal voyages with her husband had been feasible for her—which they were not because she could not leave the children behind so long and so often. So Campobello must frequently have caused Eleanor Roosevelt to feel left out, and must have provided her, too, with something pretty close to her customary diet of modest doses of pleasure and satisfaction with substantial doses of duty to be done.

APPRENTICE POLITICIAN

For some time, Franklin Roosevelt had been turning the possibility of a political career over in his mind. As the bride's uncle, Theodore Roosevelt had come up for the wedding to give Eleanor Roosevelt away, and he was so far the star of the occasion that the bride and groom had to leave the receiving line to join the crowd around the President, for want of enough company in their traditional place. As President, too, Theodore Roosevelt was much given to urging "young fellows of our sort" to enter politics in his footsteps, and the man of his name who had married his niece was not forgotten. The late Grenville Clark, who was Franklin Roosevelt's fellow clerk at the powerful firm of Carter, Ledyard, and Milburn, used to recall his astonishment when Roosevelt announced to him that he thought he might be President one day himself.

Roosevelt further explained that this would require going first to the New York state legislature in Albany, then a while in Washington, if possible as Assistant Secretary of the Navy, then the Governorship of New York, and after that the White House. This program was modeled closely on the major stages of Theodore Roosevelt's career; but the program also comprises all the main stages of Franklin Roosevelt's own career. Clark's story is exceptionally interesting, in fact, as showing that Roosevelt had already developed something of the astonishing longheadedness which served him so well.

In 1910, at any rate, the Democrats of Hyde Park's surrounding region offered Franklin Roosevelt the nomination as State Senator from Columbia, Dutchess, and Putnam Counties. Barring the small city of Poughkeepsie, which had a substantial Democratic majority, these farming counties were normally rock-ribbed Republican. Roosevelt, again showing predictive shrewdness, hired a bright red open car and campaigned endlessly through the farm areas, leaving Poughkeepsie to take care of itself. He further ran as an avowed anti-Tammany Democrat, a strong Progressive on the Theodore Roosevelt model, a friend of the farmers and an "honest government" man. It was a most shrewdly planned campaign, and he won by a majority of over a thousand votes out of 30,000 votes cast—the second Democrat ever to be sent by these counties to the State Senate.

With comparable shrewdness, Roosevelt then went on to seize the first significant opportunity offered him in Albany, where he and his wife took a big house for the first year of his two-year Senate term. To understand this opportunity, however, it is necessary to understand the New York State political pattern of those days. New York City was in the grip of Tammany Hall, and the Tammany boss, Charles F. Murphy, further had allies in the Democratic centers upstate, plus a

35

comfortable working arrangement with the state's Republican boss, William Barnes, a wily arch-conservative who was Theodore Roosevelt's bitter enemy. New York in those days also chose its U.S. Senators in the old way, by majority of a joint session of the State Senate and the State Assembly; and in 1910, Tammany boss Murphy was committed to give the U.S. Senate seat to the rich but fairly malodorous "Blue-eyed Billy" Sheehan.

Tammany was not quite as awful then as it was usually painted. The Tammany-sponsored president pro tempore of the State Senate was the young Robert F. Wagner, later to be one of the finest members of the U.S. Senate during Franklin Roosevelt's Presidency, and in the Assembly the Democratic leader was Alfred E. Smith, later to be the most effective Governor New York State ever had. But Tammany meant evil, pure, simple, and unalloyed, to every farmer in New York State and to all the "honest government" Democrats, and Boss Murphy's fairly brutal tactics had also caused a rebellion in the Brooklyn branch of the New York City organization.

In this situation, a respected Democratic Assemblyman from Brooklyn, E. R. Terry, raised the standard of revolt against Boss Murphy's choice of "Blue-eyed Billy" Sheehan for the U.S. Senate. The newly elected Roosevelt instantly rallied to the cause, and before long he and Terry had rounded up sixteen more Democratic State Senators and Assemblymen, thus denying Boss Murphy the majority that was needed to send his man to Washington. The ensuing fight was very long and distinctly complicated. But all that matters is that Franklin Roosevelt quickly made his big Albany house the permanent meeting place of the anti-Murphy, anti-Sheehan group of Democrats in the legislature; that the fight against Tammany attracted nationwide attention; and that because of his name, his youth, his looks, and his role of host at the meeting place, much of the attention focused on Roosevelt. He was even erroneously regarded as the original standard-bearer of Tammany's Democratic enemies.

In the end, the fight changed nothing except that the hapless Sheehan's nomination had to be withdrawn. Yet it was still a noteworthy fight; for it made Franklin Roosevelt a most useful statewide reputation and further gave him a good start towards a nationwide reputation. This aided him, in turn, with the voters of the three counties he represented.

Few have escaped so rapidly, or with such applause, from the dim obscurity which is the usual lot of State Senators.

The first two years in Albany paid another important dividend. Louis McHenry Howe, then an ill-paid newspaperman in Albany, had studied young Roosevelt in action, had been much impressed, and had hitched his wagon to this new star. He was a gnome-like little man, ill-dressed, even inadequately washed on occasion. Yet he had great knowledge of politics and the ways of politicians; he was fertile in brilliant devices and had a way with words; and he was untiring, too. I never knew him and have never understood him—least of all, what led him to make his own entire career out of making another man President, which is what he set out to do from the first. Perhaps he saw Franklin Roosevelt as the living embodiment of what he would have liked to be himself, and saw too that if he wanted to be a power in politics, as he most certainly did, he could only hope to gain his end through the success of this other man.

What is really significant for this essay on Roosevelt, however, is the way Roosevelt at once saw the promise of immense usefulness in the outwardly repellent although incisive and intelligent Howe, and proceeded to make the fullest use of him as long as Howe lasted. Making others useful to him as soon as the opportunity offered was one of Roosevelt's more remarkable talents. But one wonders what Mrs. James Roosevelt and her daughter-in-law thought, at least at first, about this unlikely addition to the household—which is what Louis Howe eventually became, although he had a wife and children of his own.

Howe's value was soon proven to the hilt. In 1912, when it came time to run for reelection to the State Senate, Roosevelt was in bed with typhoid fever. Howe was therefore called in for a minuscule salary, and devised and carried out an unprecedented campaign plan based on saturating Roosevelt's Senate district with craftily planned and craftily written literature of many sorts, including personal letters from the candidate—a great Howe specialty.

The Republican Party's troubles had meanwhile come to a head with Theodore Roosevelt's nomination on the independent Bull Moose-Progressive ticket. This gave the 1912 Presidential election to Woodrow Wilson, with the Bull Moose candidate in second place, while the unhappy William Howard Taft lumbered past the post a bad third.

Howe's labors and strategy, aimed at adding the Bull Moose-Progressive vote to the Democratic vote, won Franklin Roosevelt reelection to the State Senate by a fair but reduced majority.

This was important, for being reelected gave Roosevelt unchallengeable standing as one of the younger New York Democrats most deserving of consideration. Even more important, Roosevelt had come out for the New Jersey reforming Governor, Woodrow Wilson, well in advance of the Democratic convention of 1912, and had gone to Baltimore to fight hard for Wilson through this angry, suffocating, and sweat-stained gathering, which only ended when William Jennings Bryan plumped for Wilson as an anti-Wall Street man. Roosevelt expected and hoped for a reward without altogether counting on it, as one can plainly see from the fact that he took a modest apartment in Albany to replace the big house during his next State Senate term. In due course the reward came, and in just the form Roosevelt had hoped for—an offer of the Assistant Secretaryship of the Navy. So the State Senate was abandoned and the Roosevelts soon had to take a house in Washington. Roosevelt further asked Louis Howe to come along with him as his assistant at the Navy Department.

Of this Washington experience, much must be said about what happened there to the Roosevelts as human beings, but what happened to Roosevelt politically can be briefly covered. He formed a close relationship with his homespun, learned, and elderly chief, Secretary of the Navy Josephus Daniels. He did an excellent job as Assistant Secretary, too; for he endeared himself to the regular naval officers by his enthusiasm for naval power and the remarkable seamanship which he loved to display whenever he went to sea; he handled all the difficult problems of naval contracts and the Navy's labor relations with real astuteness and efficiency; and he made a major contribution to the U.S. Navy's readiness for its role in the First World War.

In 1914, he took a little time away from the Navy Department to make the only real misstep of his political career. After much havering and wavering, he entered the New York primary election for the Democratic nomination to the U.S. Senate, for New York State had meanwhile abandoned the old method of choosing U.S. Senators by a majority of the legislature. He stood as an overtly anti-Tammany candidate, moreover, which merely led Tammany bosses to offer

38

a highly respectable nominee of their own; and in the upshot Roosevelt was humiliatingly defeated in the primary. He had grown too self-confident, in truth, but he learned from his error, for he was a great learner from experience.

Thereafter he was always careful to keep his distance from Tammany, and thus to avoid the Tammany label which harmed Alfred E. Smith almost as much as his Catholicism in the 1928 Presidential election. But despite this careful distancing, Roosevelt never again bucked the New York City organization directly. He was never Tammany's choice for office; and in 1932, when Tammany strongly backed Alfred E. Smith for a second Presidential nomination, he vigorously opposed Smith and won. None the less, he never again fought Tammany head-on, so to speak, making Tammany and its wicked ways an open issue; and thus the organization never again had a good excuse for actively trying to defeat Roosevelt when voting time came.

Meanwhile, he made solid political gains as Assistant Secretary of the Navy, most conspicuously after the misstep in 1914. The main gain was a substantially increased national reputation. With constant guidance from Louis Howe and with his own sure instinct, he used his post in the Navy with great political skill and in a way that would be impossible today, when an Assistant Secretary is one of many instead of one of a kind, and has the merest ghost of the kind of responsibility that Roosevelt had. When he went to Washington, he was still no more than one promising Democrat among many. But by adroitly publicizing all that he did as Assistant Secretary of the Navy, he managed to leave Washington, not as a major figure in the Democratic Party, to be sure, but as the kind of second-rank figure who can never be counted out and always has a future before him if his luck is good and he plays his cards right.

To the foregoing only one point needs to be added, primarily because of the tendency of modern American liberals to regard Roosevelt as a father-figure, and not only in the area of domestic policy but also in the foreign field. Nothing could be more misleading than to picture Franklin Roosevelt as sharing the modern American liberal view that history is an amiable, risk-free process, and that all other powers, however much they threaten American interests, will soon become cozily nice if America's leaders merely treat America's seeming enemies as nice by nature. The items of Roosevelt's correspondence posthumously unearthed by the historians show instead that even in the years just before American entry into the First World War, he already dissented vigorously from the basic tenets of what now passes for American liberal thought about foreign affairs. Like Theodore Roosevelt, he strongly favored the Allied powers against Germany, and was converted rather early (to the alarm of Josephus Daniels) to the need for American intervention in the First World War. But this was to be expected, since this was the all but universal posture of Americans of the group he came from. More significantly, he already understood that the world was changing radically and perilously, and he therefore strongly believed that national safety must be sought by maintaining a favorable balance of power. Furthermore, he believed that every nation's policies are based on hard national interests, and he vigorously advocated a strong national defense for all these reasons. Nor did he regard the United States as an international moral policeman, especially charged with supervising the internal affairs of American allies. Roosevelt's rule for allies was stated by him: "He may be a Son of a Bitch, but he's *our* Son of a Bitch."

What happened to Roosevelt personally during his first service in Washington none the less strikes me as more interesting than what happened to him politically, partly because I believe that this side of his Washington experience affected him profoundly, and partly because it is still universally misunderstood and often grossly misrepresented.

The Roosevelts had their last two sons during their first years in Washington. Yet it also seems probable that in Washington they began to go their own ways for the first time, albeit very tentatively until a severe crisis occurred in their lives shortly before the Washington years came to an end. One reason for the divergence was simple enough. Franklin Roosevelt loved the world and its pleasures, which were offered in plenty by the small Washington in those days, where all were eager to make friends with a couple so presentable as the young Assistant Secretary of the Navy and his wife; whereas Eleanor Roosevelt already rather plainly found the world and its pleasures only intermittently enjoyable and even unpleasant on occasion. "Duty first" was just as plainly the *leitmotiv* of her first Washington experience as it was, indeed, of her entire remarkable and admirable life. One can best see how differently the husband and

40

wife approached the more worldly and pleasure-aimed side of Washington by examining their different approaches to Alice Roosevelt Longworth, Theodore Roosevelt's eldest daughter and thus another first cousin of Eleanor Roosevelt's.

Alice Longworth was one of those people who are major figures while they live, yet leave little behind except their memories. She was beautiful, witty, intelligent, and tough-minded, and she had a mortal horror of anything or anyone with the least savor of gush or sentimentality, earnest dullness or overly ostentatious virtue. Simple goodness, moreover, was by no means her favorite human quality. She preferred an ambience more complex, more scintillating, and more highly colored than the simply good are likely to generate. Since being good was always Eleanor Roosevelt's grand aim, she was not made for intimacy with her cousin, and she had somewhat feared her from childhood.

The contrast between the two cousins was wonderfully brought out, not entirely to Alice Longworth's advantage, in the period after the United States entered the First World War. The crowds of young servicemen pouring through Washington created a need. In that benighted era, there was no USO to meet the need; so volunteer ladies opened canteens. At once, Eleanor Roosevelt began working at the Red Cross canteen up to twelve hours daily. Alice Longworth, meanwhile, blithely told all and sundry that she suffered from a rare and mysterious disease she christened "canteen-elbow," and she did no war work except what she invented herself.

As a matter of course, both Roosevelts were welcomed in Washington by Alice Longworth and her husband, Nicholas Longworth, a rich, worldly, witty, self-indulgent, and already powerful Congressman. But her cousin suspected Eleanor Roosevelt of avoiding going to her house any more often than good manners required, while Franklin Roosevelt went whenever he could, often without his wife in the late afternoon, because he had a "grand time"—his phrase until the end of his life for any enjoyable experience. He further complained that his wife constantly made him go to solemn dinners of older people, where grand times were not to be had. And he even joined Alice Longworth in that invented war work above mentioned, a highly questionable experiment in amateur counter-espionage.

The victim (for that was how it turned out) was May

Ladenburg, who later became Mrs. Preston Davie and gained a certain fame as a *vivandière* of the ultra right-wing Republican Roosevelt-haters of the 1930s. As the daughter of a senior partner of the formerly German New York banking firm of Ladenburg, Thalmann and Co., Miss Ladenburg had come to Washington to see the wartime action, so to say. She had much success, too, for she was handsome and vivacious, and had taken a pleasant house centering on a big room at the rear where she entertained informally but luxuriously. Her chief admirer was Bernard M. Baruch, then head of the War Industries Board, and some fool in Naval Intelligence had formed a suspicion that Baruch was whispering the secrets of the War Industries Board into Miss Ladenburg's shell pink ear. The idea was that these secrets, passed on improperly because of long-gone Ladenburg German links, explained some of the sinkings of Allied ships in the Atlantic by German submarines.

Hard as it is to credit now, Alice Longworth and Franklin Roosevelt jointly rigged up some sort of primitive listening device so that they could eavesdrop from an adjacent stable on Baruch's teatime visits to the lady in her big room. The listeners heard nothing, of course, but the story inevitably began to go the rounds of the town. Eleanor Roosevelt was intensely and quite properly indignant about this venture by her husband and her first cousin. One may even guess that it made her bitterly angry with the supposed instigator, Alice Longworth. The anger still showed through, in fact, in the mere tone of her comment many years later: "I always thought Alice and Franklin were *most unjust* to poor May Ladenburg."

One more reminiscence of those years will be enough to complete this installment of the evidence that a divergence between husband and wife began in Washington. In this case, the evidence comes from the late Mrs. Warren Delano Robbins, whose diplomat-husband was a cousin, close friend, and former Hudson River neighbor of Franklin Roosevelt. The Robbinses were staying with the Roosevelts when the time came for one of the big private balls that were still given in Washington even after U.S. entry into the First World War. All four went to dinner and the ball together, but Eleanor Roosevelt left long before midnight, explaining that she hated dancing and would send the car back.

When the other three got home at last at nearly 4:00 a.m., they found Eleanor Roosevelt impersonating patience on a

42

monument on the doormat of the Roosevelt house. Rising from her doormat, she explained sweetly that she had "idiotcally" forgotten to bring her own door key. Her husband a bit acidly inquired why on earth she had not taken a cab back to the ball to get a key from him (for there were plenty of cabs on the street in Washington in those days). "I knew you were all having such a *glorious time*," she replied, "and I didn't want to *spoil the fun*." At this point in her story, Mrs. Robbins used to remark that she would not have "blamed Franklin if he had slapped Eleanor hard." Undeniably, the wife had made extreme use of a most insidious and infuriating feminine weapon against husbands, known in my odd tribe as "I am not angry, only a little sick at heart." (The label was the first sentence of a long-ago letter, circulated after the event, from the virtuous victim to the rich perpetrator of an unconventionally vigorous loving approach.)

The truth was, Eleanor Roosevelt was exceedingly angry, because she already suspected that her husband's late hours at the ball were entirely owing to the presence of the beautiful Lucy Mercer, later Mrs. Winthrop Rutherfurd. A great deal has been written about the relationship between Mrs. Rutherfurd and the future President—none of it accurate, except for the short and somewhat biased account by Joseph P. Lash, always a ferocious partisan of Mrs. Roosevelt. For one thing, until the very last years of her life, Eleanor Roosevelt pretended for the record that there had been no such relationship. She did so to her husband's biographer, Professor Frank Freidel of Harvard, and as proof she showed him affectionate letters written to her in Campobello while Franklin Roosevelt remained in Washington to do his wartime job.

Freidel was evidently unaware of the usual ways of husbands with absent wives in such situations. At any rate he was convinced by the letters and the denials, but entirely erroneously. How far the President had been in love with Miss Mercer during the First World War will be shown a little later. As for Mrs. Rutherfurd, in her later years after the Second World War, she lived mainly in Aiken, South Carolina, where she was visited by both the late Charles E. Bohlen and Mrs. John Hay Whitney. Bohlen had of course been the President's expert-in-residence on Russia through much of the Second World War, and to Bohlen's astonishment Mrs. Rutherfurd made it clear that the President kept none of his most intimate wartime concerns and gravest secrets from her. Mrs. Whitney had grown much attached to the President while married to his son, James Roosevelt, and Mrs. Rutherfurd knew this. To Mrs. Whitney she was therefore even more forthright, telling her that although she loved Winthrop Rutherfurd and owed him much, Franklin Roosevelt had none the less been the love of her life.

In sum, Franklin Roosevelt and Lucy Mercer were unquestionably in love with one another in Washington in that long ago wartime; but those who have suggested in print that the love affair followed the usual course of a love affair in the 1980s are every bit as erroneous as Professor Freidel. Except among a minority of "the swells"—always a small set—the ways of the group both Franklin Roosevelt and Lucy Mercer came from had no resemblance whatever to the ways of the sector of English society in which known lovers were discreetly given neighboring rooms in big country houses. Franklin Roosevelt's New York and Lucy Mercer's Maryland were very far indeed from the "King's friends" in Edward VII's England.

Miss Mercer was another "who was she," for her father, Carroll Mercer, was one of the Mercers who gave Mercersburg, Maryland, its name, and the Mercers in turn were closely related to the Carrolls, the family famous for producing the only signer of the Declaration of Independence richer than George Washington, Charles Carroll of Carrollton, as well as the first American Roman Catholic Archbishop, Charles Carroll's brother. Miss Mercer's mother was a Virginian, and may have been a Catholic convert. But they took their tone from the Maryland Catholic group to whom Carroll Mercer was linked. Catholics had been among the state's first settlers; and Maryland Catholics, like other Catholics belonging to such long-established minorities in Protestant-dominated countries, have always tended to be extra-strict and extra-devout. Mrs. Mercer and her daughter Lucy were no exceptions.

Carroll Mercer was an officer in the Marine Corps, and initially he and his wife had been more than comfortably well off. Unhappily, the money went as money will; the couple split up; and this left Mrs. Mercer and her two daughters with hardly more than a pittance. Lucy Mercer therefore became a social secretary to make a bit of badly needed money—but this in no way interfered with her success in Washington, which was insured by her looks, her charm, and her place on the "who was she" roster. She met Franklin

Roosevelt because Eleanor Roosevelt was one of the women using her as a part-time social secretary, but another kind of link soon formed. She and Roosevelt fell deeply in love.

Lucy Mercer's devout Catholicism would certainly have interfered, however, in the unlikely event that she was ever tempted to stretch the stern rules of her own upbringing by her love of Franklin Roosevelt. They danced together. They went to Alice Longworth's to tea and dinner together. They sometimes even drove together to Oatlands, the big Virginia country place of Mrs. William C. Eustis. Although she only had suspicions to go on, Eleanor Roosevelt almost certainly knew what was afoot just about as well as her Cousin Alice or her friend Edith Eustis—for each of whom she put a permanent black mark in her book because she knew their houses had been used as meeting places. Knowing, she was undoubtedly hurt very greatly, too, as anyone can surmise from the episode of the doormat, which can only be explained by an uncontrollable impulse to hurt her husband in return, in any way possible and at all costs. But that was that, beyond any reasonable doubt. To understand what really happened, in fact, it is again best to turn to *The Age of Innocence* and read of the love of Newland Archer and Countess Olenska, which also inflicted great hurts without being in the least like the love affairs described by John Updike in *Couples*.

One might leave the story there if it had ended there, but it did not. In 1918, Roosevelt came home from a European trip on Navy business with a bad case of double pneumonia, which was then a potentially fatal illness. Complete rest and seclusion were ordered for him, and Eleanor Roosevelt therefore handled his correspondence. She thus ran across letters to him from Lucy Mercer. (One cannot help wondering whether she did not look for them; for the gravely wounded always end by trying to pluck out and inspect the daggers in their bosoms.) A showdown could no longer be ducked or dodged, and she offered her husband two choices: either the marriage could continue for the children's sake, but only if he agreed to break off for good with this other woman; or else she would "give him his freedom"—she reportedly used the well-worn phrase—if that was what he wanted.

This was by no means the end of the matter, however, if tribal lore can be trusted. Her son's and daughter-in-law's difficulties were later discussed by Mrs. James Roosevelt with Mrs. Douglas Robinson. The two near-contemporaries were close friends, as I have said, and this youngest sister of Theodore and Elliott Roosevelt was not only the aunt of Eleanor Roosevelt, but also, as the latter once remarked to me, "one of the very few" senior women in the family who had "always" shown "warmth and kindness" when her niece was a most unhappy and ungainly child and young girl. She was a woman, too, who loved a good story, but her account of what Mrs. James Roosevelt told her so perfectly fits the characters of all concerned that it is worth setting down.

According to this story, then, Franklin and Eleanor Roosevelt informed his mother of the stage they had reached together. Whereat Mrs. James Roosevelt replied grimly that it was all very well for "you, Eleanor, to talk about being 'willing to give Franklin his freedom'." But she wished her son to understand quite clearly, there and then, that she "would not give him another dollar" if he left "a wife and five children for another woman." It must be understood that the threat, if made, was a far from empty one. Mrs. James Roosevelt really did have most of the money as well as title to the Hyde Park house which her son loved so dearly. Furthermore, it was too late for Franklin Roosevelt to hope to make a handsome living at the law; he was an exceptionally bad businessman, as events later proved; and he already regarded politics as his permanent career. None the less, he was entirely ready to defy his mother and to leave his wife and children if Lucy Mercer would have him as her husband.

But of course she would not have him, because she could not. As a devout Catholic, it was out of the question for her to marry a divorced man—particularly a man solely divorced in order to marry her—under the unrelenting rules of the Church as then laid down.

Many may wonder, indeed, why Franklin Roosevelt, his wife, and his mother went through such a stormy passage without realizing in advance that he could never marry Lucy Mercer while his wife still lived. He must certainly have been aware that the religious faith of the woman he loved would make it exceedingly difficult for her to marry him; but men much in love rarely accept the fact that they cannot surmount such obstacles, until they learn from hard experience that this can never be done. As for his wife and mother, Catholicism and all it meant was entirely outside their experience in those days.

The two women together cannot have counted more than

46

half a dozen believing Catholics in the combined ranks of their friends (as opposed to the ranks of their households). They also shared the prejudices of their group in a degree that may surprise those who recall only the mature Eleanor Roosevelt. In 1918 she was decidedly anti-Semitic, as her letters to her mother-in-law unpleasantly reveal; and her anti-Catholicism was so strong that it never left her, and led her into the battle against aid for parochial schools which caused her public quarrel with Cardinal Spellman of New York after the Second World War. Given these limitations, it is most unlikely that either mother or wife even dimly suspected in advance that there was no possibility whatever of Lucy Mercer marrying Franklin Roosevelt.

Be that as it may, the really striking aspect of this moving and sad story is the behavior of the three principals when the climax came. Franklin Roosevelt was ready to sacrifice both fortune and career to love. Eleanor Roosevelt did not choose to keep her husband against his will. Lucy Mercer was guided by deep religious faith and strong principles. All met this crisis in their lives, in fact, in the grandest style—to a degree that one can only admire nowadays, although their version of the grand style is likely to bewilder all too many persons in the 1980s.

The story that has now been recounted also had two sequels, which had best be told here without regard to chronology. The first sequel was Lucy Mercer's all but immediate marriage to Winthrop Rutherfurd, still a fine looking and vigorous man but almost a generation older. As his name alone would have told you in those days, he came from Edith Wharton's "apex of the pyramid." "Winthrop" was of course the surname of the first Governor of Massachusetts; for the families of the "apex" often took their given names from the surnames of other closely related clans of equal significance. Rutherfurd Stuyvesants, Stuyvesant Rutherfurds, and even triple threats like Delancey Kane Jay proliferated *ad infinitum*, and each total name was a claim in itself. As I have already said, exploring this sector of the past is like visiting Tahiti before Captain Cook.

Nor was this all, by any means. Winthrop Rutherfurd had not only been one of the two or three handsomest and most admired younger men in the late phase of old New York; he had also been famously successful with women of his own sort when this was infinitely more difficult than it is today. On a quite different level, he had also loved and been loved

47

by the beautiful Consuelo Vanderbilt. (He was the unidentified "Chevalier de la Rose" of her memoirs.) Consuelo's scheming and ruthless mother much preferred a dukedom, however, so she forced her daughter into a most unhappy marriage with the Duke of Marlborough of that day, who was in need of a great heiress. Winthrop Rutherfurd then married another considerable heiress, Alice Morton, who bore him sons and a daughter and then died.

He was therefore a widower when he married Lucy Mercer, whom he had met in the normal way in their world. He probably saw much of her too with Mrs. William C. Eustis, his first wife's sister and Lucy Mercer's friend. Like so many men who have had great success with women, he was no doubt in want, as a middle-aged widower, of another wife to settle down with. And Lucy Mercer, like so many women who have been through intense but fruitless love affairs, was perhaps in want of a husband. Moreover, her confessor, whom she trusted, urged the marriage on her.

On the eve of her engagement's announcement in the newspapers, she called Mrs. Frank Polk to ask a favor of her. Being engaged to Winthrop Rutherfurd, she felt she should not write to Franklin Roosevelt. Hence she could not notify the man she had loved, yet did not want him to learn of her engagement from a newspaper announcement; so she asked Mrs. Polk, her close friend, to tell him. Both Polks—he was Undersecretary of State after Robert Lansing moved up to replace Bryan—were close friends to the Roosevelts, and had no difficulty arranging to go to tea there. A difficulty arose, however, because Mrs. Polk could not find any excuse to get Franklin Roosevelt to herself. When leaving, she resorted to the fairly desperate expedient of telling Eleanor Roosevelt of the engagement with seeming casualness but in a voice pitched to be overheard by the two men, who were still in talk together. Roosevelt started like a horse in fear of a hornet, but there this first sequel ended, as far as the record shows.

The second sequel began much later. The Rutherfurds lived together in much contentment as long as Winthrop's health lasted. As a stepmother, the second Mrs. Rutherfurd was much loved by her stepsons and stepdaughter; she also had a daughter of her own; and while her husband lived, she sometimes corresponded with Franklin Roosevelt. She even saw him briefly when she went to Washington to visit her aging mother during his first years in the White House. But these were passing contacts without real intimacy. In 1941, however, Winthrop Rutherfurd fell ill in Aiken; she brought him to Washington for treatment; and Mrs. Eustis, who liked human drama above all, thereupon tried to arrange a meeting in the White House. Much to the disappointment of Mrs. Eustis, however, and indeed to the President's disappointment, Mrs. Rutherfurd balked at the last minute and only sent her daughter, Barbara, and stepdaughter, Alice.

A new situation arose, in fact, only after Winthrop Rutherfurd died of the illness that caused the journey from Aiken to Washington. Very naturally, the President wrote Mrs. Rutherfurd a letter of condolence in his own hand, just as the old conventions required, but perhaps a little more reminiscent than was quite conventional in such letters. She replied, of course; and in the upshot they were soon seeing one another again whenever the pressures of the war on him and her own situation permitted them to meet. Under cover of the wartime censorship-blackout of almost all the President's journeys out of Washington, he even stopped once to visit her at Allamuchy, the big Rutherfurd place in New Jersey, and she dined at the White House when Eleanor Roosevelt was on her wartime trips. There were a good many other meetings, and at the end she joined him at Warm Springs when he went there on his last journey.

To Eleanor Roosevelt's knowledge, his companions at Warm Springs were two of his cousins, Miss Laura Delano and Miss Margaret Suckley—for the evidence suggests that her husband's renewed relationship with Mrs. Rutherfurd was successfully kept from Eleanor Roosevelt until his death. The party was only completed, however, when Mrs. Rutherfurd motored to Warm Springs, bringing a painter-friend, Mme. Elizabeth Shoumatoff, who was to do a Presidential portrait. When he had his last seizure in the living room at Warm Springs, he fell back and Mrs. Rutherfurd took him in her arms; but what was coming soon was all too clear and she then left Warm Springs at once. When the time inevitably came to publish the names of those who had been with the President at the end, her name was not on the list. Perhaps more significantly, Eleanor Roosevelt also omitted any mention of Mrs. Rutherfurd's presence in the account of what happened at Warm Springs in her second autobiographical volume, *This I Remember*. Instead she added a bitter, meaning-drenched passage on her own contributions and her own deficiencies as a wife, as compared to others

49

unnamed who might have been married to Franklin Roosevelt and would have been wives of another sort.

I have told this whole story at such length, not only because it seems to me moving and creditable in the main to all the principal actors, and has never been properly told before, but also, and above all, because the signs suggest that it had pretty nearly as great a role in Franklin Roosevelt's life and career as his tragic infantile paralysis. To begin with, it is a reasonable surmise that his wartime love affair, profoundly and forever resented by Eleanor Roosevelt, caused their relationship to be transformed for good from a normal marriage into the highly successful working partnership many people will still remember. Much more important, as my mother always believed, and so do I, his disappointment in a strong and strongly felt love did much to banish the "feather duster" side of Franklin Roosevelt, and to deepen, toughen, and mature his character and personality even prior to his paralysis.

It must be understood that the girls he danced with as a very young fellow, who called him "feather duster," were neither alone nor as frivolous as they now sound in their opinion of him. He was not a man who had many close men friends of his own sort, and most of these had lived on the Hudson River and were his boyhood playmates. But there were others as well, such as the future leader of the American foreign service, William Phillips, a cool and extremely astute judge of men. Where their opinions of him as a young man are recorded, as the opinion of Phillips happens to have been, there is always the same note of astonishment about what Franklin Roosevelt became.

The friends of his youth regarded him, even in the wartime years in Washington, as a high-spirited, pleasant companion, full of energy and ambition, a good fellow in all respects, but fairly superficial and wholly without the strength and largeness of character, the depth of judgment and the other qualities that are needed to make a great man, or at least a man both great and good. In short, one of the central problems facing anyone dealing with Franklin Roosevelt's personal history is just what made him the man he became. His tragic bout with polio of course completed this harsh job of man-making, but it seems highly likely that the job had been well begun already by his bitter disappointment in love. On these points, however, intuition and probability are the only available guides once all the facts have been set forth, as they have been here.

50

THE CRUCIBLE YEARS

Disappointments in love, however bitter and maturing, rarely end the careers of vigorous and active men in their thirties; and both Franklin and Eleanor Roosevelt went forward, outwardly untroubled, from the crisis in their lives caused by his love for Mrs. Rutherfurd. In 1919 they made an official trip together to Europe, where they saw something of peacemaking in Paris from the fringes of the Versailles conference. When they returned, he began to wind up his affairs at the Navy, for he was already convinced the Democrats had only a slim chance of victory in the 1920 Presidential election. None the less, he was careful to go on keeping himself before the party and the public, most notably with a speech to the Democratic National Committee's meeting in Chicago in 1919. The Attorney General, A. Mitchell Palmer, who saw himself as a Presidential candidate, was the official keynoter, and hoped to be the center of attention with one of his resounding Red-baiting speeches. Instead, Roosevelt captured the spotlight with an even more resounding progressive speech, lambasting the Republicans for being captives of their own Old Guard, and urging the Democratic Party to continue as "a progressive Democracy." The speech was not unimportant, for one of those impressed by Roosevelt's message and performance was Governor James M. Cox of Ohio, who was a really serious Presidential candidate, soon to receive the Democratic nomination.

The Democratic convention of 1920 met in San Francisco in a melancholy mood, for President Wilson had been hopelessly incapacitated by his stroke, and as soon as the war was over the fires of partisanship had been stoked up by the Republicans. The ins and outs of the convention were intricate, as always in Democratic rallies of the period before Franklin Roosevelt as President finally struck down his party's two-thirds rule for Presidential nominations. But all that matters is that Cox got the nomination and then saw to it that Roosevelt got the Vice Presidential nomination.

What followed was Franklin Roosevelt's first national campaign, and one of the more remarkable national campaigns among all those he made—simply because of his refusal to be discouraged. The outcome of the election was already close to a foregone conclusion, and was so regarded by Roosevelt himself—except in those moments of irrational optimism which come to all campaigners. Yet Roosevelt cheerfully and tirelessly barnstormed across the country on his campaign train, neglecting no chance to appeal to all possible voters along the routes chosen for him; and in this manner he enormously extended his already considerable knowledge of the United States and greatly widened his range of acquaintance and network of friendships among Democratic leaders in many states. Thus he further enhanced his standing and political reputation in his own party, even though the campaign ended with the expected landslide for Warren Gamaliel Harding and the Republican Party.

Despite his efforts, Roosevelt after this election looked remarkably like another specimen of a familiar American political type—the attractive young man who makes politics his profession, comes up fast at first, and then runs into a dead end and spends the rest of his life regretting former glories that everyone else soon forgets. By any reasonable test, he had literally nowhere to go as a politician. Neither of the New York seats in the U.S. Senate was conveniently open. The redoubtable Al Smith had an obvious right to run for Governor in 1922. And any lesser office was too much of a come-down to consider. Consequently, Roosevelt went back to the law in a fairly dilatory way, and also branched out into business.

In his years out of office, he entered into two successive legal partnerships, first with his former fellow law clerk Grenville T. Emmet and his friend Langdon P. Marvin, and then with the more political Basil O'Connor. In terms of work done and money earned, neither partnership counted for much in his life and both may be ignored hereafter. His experiments with the role of businessman similarly continued, with a long intermission for his illness, until he won the Governorship in 1928; but what little needs saying about

Roosevelt the businessman may again be set down here. In brief, he was as misguided as a businessman as he was astute as a politician. The great speculative boom of the 1920s soon developed, and he repeatedly entangled himself, mainly by letting his name be used, in ambitious but ill-conceived speculative ventures. He was probably lucky to escape from these without damage to his reputation or personal fortune. He was even luckier to have a part-time, rather routine, but fairly well paid regular job.

The job was the vice-presidency of the Fidelity and Deposit Company of Maryland, a surety bonding concern controlled by his friend, the rich Baltimorean Van Lear Black. He appears to have done well as head of this company's New York office, the relatively undemanding post Black provided for him. The post must have been important to him at the time, too, because of the salary of $25,000 a year, and because of the appearance of being occupied. Yet it still deserves no more than a footnote in any account of Roosevelt's life.

Meanwhile, one of the indisputable turning points in his life was his attack of infantile paralysis, which occurred at Campobello in August 1921. After his defeat for the Vice Presidency, he had carried a heavy schedule of public and semi-public engagements and had done all the other things, in addition to his legal and business commitments, that all politicians out of office always do when they are aiming not to be forgotten. He was a recognizably tired man when he sailed for Campobello on Van Lear Black's yacht, Sabalo. Black's captain did not know the Northern waters well; the weather was dirty; and Roosevelt had a long and tiring battle to pilot Sabalo to a safe anchorage in Welchpool Harbor in the Bay of Fundy. The next day he exhausted himself superintending all the work of a major fishing expedition on Sabalo's motor-tender, and he also made a misstep on deck and thus drenched himself in the freezing waters of the Bay. On the following day, home at Campobello, he exhausted himself in much the same way, went swimming in the freezing water with two of his boys, and then jogged home, two miles away, still in his wet bathing suit. He believed in later life that the polio had probably begun to develop before he left Sabalo, and this would not be surprising in view of the physical tests he had been inflicting on himself; but the disease came into the open only after he got home from swimming with his sons.

53

The story of the polio—the original misdiagnosis by a local doctor; the belatedly correct diagnosis by a specialist; the grim moment when Roosevelt had to face the fact that he might be paralyzed for life; and all that followed—has been so often told it is not worth retelling in detail. But there are a few points of such significance that they need to be stressed.

To begin with, it is not widely realized, even now, that the disease subjected Roosevelt to acute pain long after the actual infection passed. The parts of his body that were mainly affected remained inflamed for months, and the inflammation and the inevitable muscular adjustments and distortions at first made even bedbound passivity near-torture for him. As for the cruel but inevitable journey from Campobello to New York, it hardly bears thinking about, and the surviving contemporary descriptions are even distressing to read.

Yet from first to last and whether in public or in private—even with his wife and mother, his children and his nurses and doctors—he never failed to put a smiling, gallant front on his plight. In short, the disease revealed that he possessed a supply of sheer guts so large that even those closest to him were surprised and admiring.

His supply of guts again served him well when it came time to try to deal with the heavy handicaps the polio had imposed on him. His approach was quite simply to refuse, and refuse for years on end, to acknowledge that the handicaps could be permanent. He exercised indefatigably, building up the broad shoulders, the powerful arms, and the barrel chest which all will remember who recall the man as he was in his years of national leadership. He also tried cure after cure, beginning at a special institution for polio sufferers and others with muscular difficulties in Massachusetts, and ending at last at Warm Springs.

When he discovered Warm Springs, it was a hopelessly run-down old-fashioned Southern spa; and he put two-thirds of his private fortune—no less than $200,000—into rehabilitating the place and making it permanently available for his own use and for others in need. The warm-water pool where he swam was almost all that remained of the old resort as he had found it, but exercise in the pool benefited him greatly; he even discovered that, with the support of the warm water, he could walk again despite the extreme weakness of his legs. So he hoped to reach the stage of walking without the water to support him.

In reality, of course, the hope of walking again was delusive. He learned to use his upper body's new strength to hoist himself from a special light wheelchair he had made into any chair he wished to occupy for work or for talk; he had a small car rebuilt in such a way that he could drive without using foot pedals, and drive he did at Hyde Park and Warm Springs; and he learned to stand erect for considerable periods, albeit not without constant discomfort, nor without the help of a heavy steel brace to keep his legs from buckling under him. It was always so painful to him that great self-control was needed to keep a smiling face, but with this price paid, with more help from the heavy brace, and with a strong arm to lean on, he even managed in the end to walk fairly short distances without crutches, as would plainly be desirable on great public occasions.

To all intents, however, he remained the physical prisoner of his still-paralyzed legs until the end of his life, needing assistance from others at every turn, forced to train himself to remain for hours on end wherever he had settled himself for work or for amusement, and in general immobilized by his disease once he had made the great effort to arrange himself in any new environment until the time came for another move, when he would need help again—unless it was just a matter of hoisting himself back into his wheelchair and propelling himself to the luncheon or dinner table.

Guts, optimism about finding a way out, and the kind of tough obstinacy that refuses to accept defeat, are all exceptionally useful qualities for a national leader to possess, not least in dangerous times. Obviously, the ordeal of his paralysis did not create these qualities in Roosevelt. They must always have been there, *in posse* so to say, under the high-spirited but sometimes trivial-seeming surface of Roosevelt as a young man. But it is fairly clear that these qualities were forcibly exercised and developed by Roosevelt's ordeal, just as his upper body and arms were enormously developed by the bodily exercises he did to escape the prison of paralysis. What was *in posse* before was therefore *in esse* when the time of need came.

Hence guts, rational optimism, and tough obstinacy about accepting defeat were added in full measure to Roosevelt's extreme wiliness, his magical sense of political timing, and his remarkable astuteness in avoiding showdowns until a showdown was likely to produce a satisfying result. The mere recital of these qualities amounts to a recipe for as formidable a political leader as the United States has known in the 20th century—which was precisely what Roosevelt became.

In a curious, perhaps cruel way, the seeming tragedy of Franklin Roosevelt's polio must in truth be seen in the light of hindsight as a great gain for him. It is a rule of life in this weary world that few experiences an individual can encounter are ever wholly wasted—unless the individual is destroyed thereby; and for an intelligent and resilient man even the harshest survived experiences are somehow liberating. Not only did Roosevelt's polio finish the job of making him the man he became, which had been begun by his strong but disappointed love. In addition, although I think this has not been suggested before, the paralysis most unexpectedly helped him to become Governor of New York and then President of the United States.

It is another rule of life that ambitious men who feel blocked and hedged in always tend to commit follies, and politicians in this situation commit worse follies than almost anyone. Roosevelt was in just this predicament from 1920 until 1928, and the resulting temptations to make wrong judgments might well have been too strong for him if he had been a well man. For instance, the frustrations of being in a dead end might well have led him to challenge Alfred E. Smith's claim to the Governorship in 1922. But in 1922 his condition left Roosevelt no choice, so he was the leader of the New York Democrats who pressed Smith to make the fight, and he gained greatly thereby. More generally, he gained greatly in national stature in a positive way by the courage and style he showed in his crippled condition. His big chance in this respect came at the Democratic convention of 1924.

The convention met in New York, without air-conditioning of course, in fearful summer heat, and in near-permanent deadlock too because of the party's two-thirds rule. Under the two-thirds rule, a Presidential nominee could not be chosen without the support of two-thirds of the convention delegates. It was a rule dear to the Southern leaders, and also to the Northern big-city bosses, for it gave any substantial minority a veto power over the Democratic nomination.

The candidate of what may be called the rural Democrats and most of the Southerners was William Gibbs McAdoo,

Wilson's former Secretary of the Treasury as well as his son-in-law, who had campaigned as a bone Dry, an anti-Tammany man, and a pseudo-populist. A majority of the delegates favored Al Smith, an unashamed, all-out Wet, with a record as a genuinely progressive and reforming Governor. ("Dry" and "Wet"—for those with short memories—meant for and against the Prohibition amendment, then thought to be God-ordained in rural America and loathed in the cities.) Hence the combination of Smith's wetness, his Catholicism, and his Tammany links made him the spokesman for Satan to many Democratic delegates, thus in turn making the McAdoo votes rock solid. And as neither of the leading candidates had even close to a two-thirds majority, an interminable deadlock was inevitable.

In the hope of escaping from this trap, Al Smith turned to Franklin Roosevelt, as he did again when he needed help in 1928. One may guess that Smith always regarded the younger man as a political dilettante, not to be taken seriously because he had not come up the hard way. This was a bad mistake, as Smith learned after the 1928 election. But at least Smith could tell when a man was likely to be useful; in 1924 he had a notion Roosevelt might just turn the trick for him; and there is no doubt Roosevelt helped Smith enormously at the convention, which was held in the old Madison Square Garden.

The Garden was already glaring with lights, and every delegate was also running with sweat, when Roosevelt rose from his place in the New York delegation and slowly made his way to the platform, in order to put Smith's name in nomination. He was still a young-looking, very handsome man in those days, and he had to reach the speakers' stand and make his speech on crutches, for this was before he had mastered the task of seeming to walk and stand almost unaided. The distance to the podium was great; covering it on crutches was a heavy effort for him; but he managed to make it seem effortless. The performance, by a man known to have been totally immobilized by paralysis less than three years earlier, was stirring in itself. The "Happy Warrior" speech—for so it was always remembered, from the proud epithet bestowed on Al Smith—was still more stirring. The phrase "Happy Warrior" was added to the speech by one of Smith's strategists, but Roosevelt wrote the main parts of the speech himself, most notably the plea to the Democratic delegates to "keep first in your hearts and minds the words of Abraham Lincoln, 'With malice toward none, with charity for all.'"

The ensuing outburst of emotion in the hall was tremendous and (for once in a way at a national convention) strongly sustained by genuine feeling. For a moment, it was a case of "e'en the ranks of Tuscany could scarce forebear to cheer." But the next day, the ranks of Tuscany had reformed well enough to defeat a resolution condemning the Ku Klux Klan, then riding very high in the South and parts of the Midwest. Roosevelt was also Smith's floor-leader, but despite his best efforts the deadlock continued until the 93rd ballot. Roosevelt then ended the long orgy of partisan squalor and mounting factional rage with another moving, much applauded speech, announcing that Al Smith had decided to withdraw his candidacy if McAdoo did likewise. The end was a futile, foredoomed compromise on John W. Davis a few ballots later.

Before this anticlimax, not a few wiseacres had suggested that the delegates might do worse than compromise on Franklin Roosevelt instead of Smith. This was balderdash, for he was debarred by his commitments to Smith from any such arrangement; but there is still no doubt that it reflected an important reality—the great new gain in stature in his party and the country which Roosevelt achieved by the way he handled his tasks at Madison Square Garden. The gain was not merely political, either. Thereafter the writers of poison-pen letters might circulate vicious stories about Roosevelt's physical condition—as they were later to do for years on end, when they took to hinting that his paralysis was really caused by syphilis. Yet there was never again any serious question about his mental vigor and physical ability to withstand the burdens of leadership. This even continued to be true when perhaps there should have been questions, during his candidacy for a fourth term in the White House in 1944.

Thus what happened at the convention in 1924 prepared the way for what happened to Roosevelt in 1928. In that year there was no question of the rural Democrats standing in the way of Al Smith's nomination on the Democratic ticket; but there was a serious question about whether the Democrats could carry New York State if Smith left the Governorship to run for the Presidency. By then Roosevelt believed, rightly or wrongly, that his long visits to Warm Springs for rest, combined with incessant exercise in the pool and else-where, were close to restoring his power to walk. Or did he claim to believe this in order to have an excuse for forcing Smith and his strategists to beg him, over and over, to abandon Warm Springs in order to save New York State for the Democrats by running for Governor himself? With a man like Roosevelt, one can never know the answer to such questions with certainty. One can only note that having been begged to run by Smith with the active but unwilling support of Tammany, he was freed of any obligation to Tammany or Smith; yet he ended in contented possession of the Governorship of New York, which he had always wanted very much as a necessary and major step in his career.

In the Presidential campaign Al Smith went down to defeat by Herbert Hoover—and by the religious prejudice then rife among Southern Democrats. Roosevelt won narrowly in New York, meanwhile, thus running ahead of Smith in his own state. He received a fine inheritance too, for Smith—the best Governor of that era—had all but miraculously managed to carry through a root-and-branch reform and modernization of the antiquated machinery of New York State government. Smith therefore expected Roosevelt to be much guided by his own favorite advisers, Robert Moses and the able Belle Moskowitz. The trouble between the two men started there and then, in fact, for Smith was exceedingly angry when Roosevelt politely but coolly indicated that he preferred to have advisers and assistants of his own choosing.

Of Roosevelt as Governor it is almost enough to say that he poked no political hornets' nest for ideological reasons, yet was humane, liberal, efficient, and so popular that he won reelection by an impressive majority in 1930. He was by no means so memorable a Governor as his predecessor had been (at any rate in my opinion), but a memorable performance in the narrow confines of Albany was not what Roosevelt was really aiming for. He was aiming, rather, for the White House itself, and thus what really matters about his Governorship was what prepared him for the fight for the Democratic nomination in 1932 and his first years as President thereafter.

One of his ways of preparing the road to the White House was to choose the issues he stressed and the adversaries he fought as Governor with exceptional adroitness. The first of his programs to become law gave aid to the farmers of New

59

York State, where the number of family farms was already declining year after year. Fortunately for Roosevelt, wheat and the other large-scale commodity crops hardly mattered in New York, so he could—and did—become the farmers' friend without dangerously committing himself to one or another of the violently conflicting nationwide farm programs then being advocated in depressed farming areas of the Midwest and Plains states.

Again, he took a firm and successful stand in favor of public development of New York State's rich waterpower resources. This was not an easy thing to do at first, for big business still wielded big influence until the stock market crash of 1929 turned into the depression of 1930, and in 1928 big business was seeking control of the waterpower resources for the large public utility combines sponsored by J. P. Morgan and Co. and others. Yet the promise of cheap electric rates had much appeal to the middle-class, mostly Republican, voters of upstate New York; and Roosevelt took his stand on waterpower and made it stick in such a way that he kept plenty of friends in the New York City financial district. He handled the New York City Democratic organization with the same astuteness too. The Bronx branch of the organization, led by the able Edward J. Flynn, was growing in importance and was also semi-independent of Tammany Hall in Manhattan. Roosevelt, who liked and trusted Flynn, therefore made the Bronx leader Secretary of State of New York. Meanwhile, however, he was careful to keep his distance from Tammany and the branch in Brooklyn, although he never again made the mistake of fighting Tammany Hall head-on, as I have said.

His first and probably his most worrying decision in fact was the one concerning Al Smith rather than Tammany Hall. He reappointed most of the members of Smith's excellent and unusually nonpartisan Cabinet, and he promoted Frances Perkins from a subordinate place in the state government to be his Industrial Commissioner—the equivalent of Secretary of Labor—thereby naming the best person for a big job, and pleasing not only Mrs. Perkins's friend, Eleanor Roosevelt, but also the powerful faction of social workers from whom Frances Perkins came, as well as those who wished to see women in positions of greater public responsibility, all in one neat stroke. But Roosevelt drew the line at doing what Smith above all wanted him to do: continuing Robert Moses, who had been Smith's Secretary of State, and

Smith's domineering but brilliant personal assistant, Belle Moskowitz, in their former positions as the Governor's chief policy advisers. Moses was left with the State Parks to develop, which he did with an imperial reach and efficiency, but Mrs. Moskowitz was dropped for good. Smith was unforgivingly angry; for he had somewhat strangely expected the Roosevelt Governorship to continue the Smith Governorship under another name.

Roosevelt's primary motive was certainly the simple desire for complete independence and for this he was ready to defy Smith. In addition, what Al Smith had expected of Roosevelt suggests that Smith had no inkling of the peculiar relationship that had grown up between Franklin Delano Roosevelt and Louis McHenry Howe. If Mrs. Moskowitz had been accepted as a chief Roosevelt policy adviser, she and Howe would have been at each other's throats in a week.

Throughout the years of Roosevelt's convalescence, Howe never ceased to regard the other man's career as his own. He was about to strike out for himself when Roosevelt suffered the polio attack; he was called back immediately; and then responded to the call without hesitation. Thereafter, he served continuously in the combined roles of chief of staff, public relations man, and political strategist. He not only helped Roosevelt to return to his business concerns and law practice far sooner than had been thought possible; he also attended to Roosevelt's ever-growing correspondence with Democratic leaders outside New York, and he was constantly preoccupied with calculations of the right time for Roosevelt to return actively to public life. He did not think 1928 the right time, but when the decision was made, he assumed the entire backroom management of Roosevelt's political campaign for the Governorship.

In sum, Howe had given up his own life for Roosevelt's needs, to the extent of spending long periods at Hyde Park, where he had his own room, and then returning to his wife and family as though on holiday. In the circumstances, Roosevelt would have been inhuman and unfeeling to confront Louis Howe with a rival in the person of Mrs. Moskowitz, whom Eleanor Roosevelt disliked and Howe probably rightly distrusted for her complete attachment to Al Smith. Furthermore, Roosevelt saw Howe from the first as the nucleus of an organization discreetly dedicated to winning the White House for his chief, as Howe had always

61

planned; and this was just what Howe became as soon as Roosevelt had won reelection to the Governorship by a dramatically increased majority in 1930.

That majority was important in itself. Running against an inept Republican, Charles H. Tuttle, with a Prohibitionist also in the field to appeal to the more rockbound, puritanical upstaters, Roosevelt carried New York State by 725,000 votes, a staggering overall plurality, which included an equally notable plurality of 167,000 votes in the Republican upstate area. It was important, too, that in his first two years in Albany Roosevelt had proved his political skill as Governor, actually circumventing and often defeating the heavy Republican majority in the state legislature without any show of Al Smith's abrasive combativeness. And it was important, again, that he had positioned himself squarely with the liberal wing of the Democratic Party—he had now begun to call himself "liberal" rather than "progressive"—without overly enraging the conservative Democrats or estranging the Southern Democrats, who were more rural-populist than truly conservative in those days.

Being Damp (which meant advocating local option on the question of Prohibition), Roosevelt was far more acceptable in the South and the rural Midwest than an all-out Wet like Al Smith. As the farmers' Eastern friend, he had nationwide appeal to farm groups, and as an advocate of public power, he was strong with the Republicans who still belonged to the Theodore Roosevelt wing of their party and with Democrats of the same kidney. If it had not been for the two-thirds rule controlling the Democratic convention, he would have been the all but certain Democratic Presidential nominee for 1932 by the end of 1930. As it was, Louis Howe and the others in the small but well-planned organization promoting Roosevelt for the Presidency still had their work cut out for them, but they must have gained confidence from the fact that he had now become the outstanding Democratic Governor in the country. In those days, it should also be remembered, any successful Governor of New York, then much the most populous state, automatically acquired a special claim to his party's Presidential nomination.

In those days, however, there were also enough remnants of the older American political tradition of the office seeking the man to make too early an open candidacy most unwise. Even after the 1930 Governorship election, Roosevelt almost certainly admitted to no one but Louis

Howe and Eleanor Roosevelt that he had already decided to seek the Democratic Presidential nomination in 1932. The decision was made as soon as the votes in the state were counted, but it was a secret—albeit an increasingly open secret as time went on. Insiders guessed what was coming, in fact, when Howe promptly moved to New York to open what can only be called an office for propaganda and correspondence.

The correspondence, which Howe prepared and Roosevelt signed, covered the entire network of nationwide friendships with other Democrats formed by Roosevelt during his long political experience, and this Howe-Roosevelt network was also widely extended as the opportunity opened. The propaganda comprised many kinds of releases and other literature, all carefully designed to emphasize Roosevelt's promise as a Democratic Presidential candidate. Nor was that all. Howe would turn up at Albany or Hyde Park whenever a serious decision had to be made, or Roosevelt would see him in New York. He continued to function, in fact, as Roosevelt's chief adviser on political strategy.

That left only one gap in the embryo organization aside from fund-raising, which mainly came later. Every Presidential campaign always needs a traveling salesman to test local sales resistance or the opposite, and to round up all possible commitments of support across the country. Roosevelt's first choice was the Bronx boss, Ed Flynn, but Flynn probably rightly considered himself insufficiently outgoing for the job and preferred to remain as Secretary of State of New York. Roosevelt then turned to a leading New York Democrat, the party chairman of Rockland County, James A. Farley. It was an ideal choice, for Jim Farley had every qualification for the task in hand.

As an Irish Catholic, he could talk on equal terms with the big-city bosses. Yet he had no Tammany links; he neither drank nor smoked; he was a man of sterling honesty and great charm; and he could also do business with perfect comfort with rural, Dry, Southern, and other Democratic leaders of the groups that had tended to vote Republican rather than support Al Smith in 1928. So Farley began his first cross-country trip, initially in the guise of an "Elk on a tour" (he was a leading Elk), and great numbers of key Democratic leaders in many states were soon enrolled in the Farley correspondence network, supplementing the Howe-Roosevelt network. Almost all the credit for securing the Democratic nomination for Franklin D. Roosevelt should in fact be divided about equally between Farley and Howe, except for the major share which must be allocated to Roosevelt himself.

Initially, it was a ticklish business, all the same. To begin with, Roosevelt had troubles in his own backyard. For one thing, the playboy Mayoralty of James J. Walker had caused corruption to run wild in New York City. An old-style Tammany scandal was the last thing Roosevelt wanted or needed. Such a scandal was plainly in the making; yet Roosevelt was also sensibly reluctant to begin another frontal anti-Tammany assault, for Tammany Hall was still the most powerful single Democratic organization in his own state. For the time being—until after the Democratic convention in 1932, in fact, when he dismissed Mayor Walker for cause—he had to content himself with allowing the charges of gross misdoing in New York City to be explored by other investigators, above all the able and ambitious Samuel Seabury. Rejecting the showy role of chief investigator for himself was another proof of Roosevelt's long-headedness.

Then, too, Roosevelt in his second term as Governor of New York had to deal with the whole new order of problems created by the Depression that had followed the stock market crash of 1929. For both crash and Depression, Roosevelt had been utterly unprepared. The main reason Louis Howe had not wanted Roosevelt to stand for Governor as early as he did was his expectation that as late as 1932 "Republican prosperity" would reduce the Democratic Presidential nomination to an empty honor. There is every reason to believe Roosevelt shared Howe's expectation, and only refused to heed Howe's advice because he realized that the kind of chance pressed on him by Al Smith in 1928 was not likely to come twice. Being unprepared for the Depression and its cruel consequences, Roosevelt was not quick off the mark in seeking to alleviate the ever more widespread and deep-reaching human misery in his state. But at least he was rather quicker off the mark than any other state Governor or the unfortunate President Hoover. And although his measures seem ludicrously inadequate stopgaps in the light of hindsight, it must also be remembered that they were bolder measures than anyone else took.

Perhaps the most noteworthy measure was the establish-

Yearbook photo, Groton School, April 1900.   1

Early days

FDR was born in the Roosevelt family home in Hyde Park, New York, on 30 January 1882. His first picture was taken seven weeks later on the day of his christening.

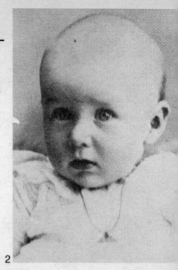

2

On a visit to Washington, D.C., the 5-year-old Franklin was made to wear a clan suit for a pair of studio photos with his father and mother. He seems distinctly unhappy in his Scottish costume. James was then 59, Sara 33.

Growing up in Hyde Park

In his early teens, FDR was bitten by the camera bug. He is seen posing beside a tripod-mounted vintage Kodak on a visit to the Delano family home at Fair Haven, Massachusetts, in September 1897.

Groton

FDR entered Groton at the late age of 14. The Massachusetts prep school, founded in 1889, was already an established way-station for boys from old and socially respectable families en route to one of the Ivy League colleges. Over the four years at Groton, FDR's grades averaged out at a B level. But book learning was only part of the Groton experience. On the next page, FDR is seen in two extracurricular activities: on the sidelines as a member of the school's second football squad (in white turtleneck, front row) and in the annual play given by the senior class (FDR, right, plays the part of Uncle Bopaddy, while his good friend Eugene Van Rensselaer Thayer is the curly-haired Poppytop). The top hat and dress jacket belonged to father James. Above, the last family portrait, taken in Poughkeepsie in May 1899, soon after FDR had returned home from his third year at prep school. James Roosevelt was then already ill; he died on 8 December 1900.

GROTON SCHOOL,
GROTON, MASS.

Report of *F. Roosevelt* 14 *years*

for the month ending *Dec. 9, 1896*

Rank in Class of *19 boys* *4*

		DIVISION AVERAGE	EXAMINATION MARK
Latin.			
	Composition,		
Greek.			
	Composition,		
	Trigonometry,		
Mathematics.	Geometry,		
	Algebra,		
	Arithmetic,		
	Literature,		
English.	Composition,		
	Grammar,		
	Reading,		
French,			
German,			
History,			
Science,			
Physics,			
Sacred Studies,			
Penmanship,			
Neatness,			
Decorum,			
AVERAGE MARK FOR THE MONTH,			
AVERAGE MARK FOR THE TERM,			

REMARKS. *Very good. He starts well and is an intelligent + faithful scholar — a good boy.*

E. Peabody

8

9

10

Harvard

At the turn of the twentieth century, Harvard was—as it had been for some 250 years—a magnet for the scions of America's most distinguished families. With his good looks and impeccable connections, FDR fell into the swim easily, making the social rounds with aplomb, if not exactly distinguishing himself as a scholar. Significantly, his choice of courses emphasized the social sciences, but in the end he emerged from his years at Harvard with no better than a C average. An indifferent athlete, he threw his extracurricular energies into the undergraduate daily paper, *The Harvard Crimson*. He "worked like a dog" and was rewarded in his junior year by being elected its president and editor-in-chief. Here he poses with the *Crimson* staff.

13

ummer holidays

acations during FDR's Harvard years were occasions for refree relaxation at the various summer homes belonging members of the clan. Opposite, the famous smile is on ew as FDR (in straw boater and striped shirt) romps with usins and friends at the Delano country estate, Steen Vatje, in 1902. Above, the camera has caught him cruising e Bay of Fundy on the family yacht *Half Moon II* (1904). this photo, taken just after his final year at Harvard, the oosevelt we all recognize has definitively emerged.

Cousin Eleanor

During his last year at Harvard, FDR had fallen in love with his fifth cousin, Anna Eleanor Roosevelt, daughter of Elliott and Anna Hall Roosevelt. Eleanor was born on 11 October 1884, and was thus nearly three years younger than FDR. He had known her since she was a baby, but the relationship blossomed into romance in 1903, shortly after Eleanor's "coming out" party in New York. Their engagement was announced in November of that year.

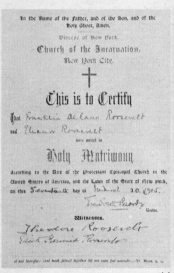

14

The marriage took place at the home of Eleanor's cousin, Mrs. Henry Parish, in New York City on 17 March 1905. President Theodore Roosevelt, Eleanor's uncle, who had come up from Washington to give the bride away, signed the marriage certificate. Eleanor posed for a studio portrait in her satin bridal gown, but strangely there are no photos of the wedding party itself. FDR was then enrolled at Columbia Law School, and it was not until June that the couple left for a honeymoon abroad. In Venice, Eleanor dutifully held her husband's straw hat while FDR snapped his bride in a gondola (July 1905).

16

17

The young lawyer

Soon after joining the Wall Street law firm of Carter, Ledyard, and Milburn in 1907, FDR drafted a jocular note on his new letterhead advertising his "unexcelled facilities for carrying on every description of legal business." In fact, his work there was quite routine, and for the first year unpaid.

But in the bustle of downtown New York he began to rub shoulders with the politicians and would-be politicians who were often to be encountered in and around the courts.

FRANKLIN D. ROOSEVELT
COUNSELLOR AT LAW
54 WALL STREET
NEW YORK

I beg to call your attention to my unexcelled facilities for carrying on every description of legal business. Unpaid bills a specialty. Briefs on the liquor question furnished free to ladies. Race suicides cheerfully prosecuted. Small dogs chloroformed without charge. Babies raised under a [...] care of expert grandmothers etc. etc. etc.

Meanwhile there was a family to raise. The circular photo, from 1908, shows the young parents with baby James and 2-year-old Anna.

19

An opening into political life came in 1910, when Democratic leaders in his own Dutchess County urged FDR to run for State Senator. He waged a strenuous campaign. To cover the 5,000-square-mile district, the young candidate traveled incessantly by car and train, usually in company with Eleanor, stopping at every crossroads village en route.

FDR campaigned on the issue of bossism versus clean government, and he did his utmost to minimize the stigma of running as a Democrat in staunchly Republican territory. He would make an average of ten speeches a day, principally in small farming communities. To everyone's complete astonishment, Roosevelt defeated his well-entrenched Republican opponent.

21

22

Off duty

While the legislature was
in session, the Roosevelts
lived in Albany, the state
capital, but during the long
summer recess they
moved to the family home
at Campobello. The photo
of FDR, Eleanor, Anna on
her pony, and Sara was
taken there in 1911. Sara
was always on hand, and
the presence of this formidable and domineering
materfamilias cannot
have been easy on the still
shy and unassertive
Eleanor.

23

Assistant Secretary of the Navy

n March 1913, FDR was appointed to the post of Assistant
Secretary of the Navy. For the next seven years he threw him-
elf into the routines of administering America's growing
navy. "I get my fingers into everything," he said, "and there's
no law against it." The job entailed frequent visits to navy
yards and bases, usually in the company of an admiral or two,
and sometimes with Eleanor as well. Occasionally there were
official ceremonies to perform, such as launching the battleship *Tennessee* at the Brooklyn Navy Yard.

24

World War I

Germany's mounting submarine warfare in the Atlantic had convinced FDR that the United States must become involved. Josephus Daniels, Secretary of the Navy, recalls him bursting into his office in the autumn of 1916 exclaiming, "We've got to get into this war." The United States did in April 1917. Sorely tempted at first to enlist, Roosevelt was persuaded that he could serve his country best by remaining at his post in Washington. It was there that he participated in a big Liberty Loan rally on 14 April 1918. With him in the photo taken on this occasion are Douglas Fairbanks and Mary Pickford and (kneeling) Marie Dressler and Charlie Chaplain. The lady clutching a fur scarf at right is Mary Pickford's mother.

On 9 July 1918, FDR left on a mission to Europe. He visited the front and watched the Sixth United States Gun Battery shelling the German lines seven kilometers away. Later he inspected the U.S. Naval Air Station in Pauillac in the Bordeaux wine country, reviewing the men stationed there. To the enlisted men he said: "It is hard for me to go back to a dull office job in Washington after having visited the lines where our boys are making history."

In the Washington swim

Although an Assistant Secretary of the Navy was only a small fish in the Washington pond, FDR quickly began to make an impression in high circles. He was tapped for minor ceremonial occasions, such as the Flag Day celebrations on 14 June 1913, when Roosevelt (far right) shared the platform with William Jennings Bryan, Josephus Daniels, President Wilson, Henry Breckinridge (Assistant Secretary of War), and William Phillips (Assistant Secretary of State). And though Wilson conspicuously failed to support FDR's doomed attempt to fight Tammany Hall in the New York State primary election of 1914 the defeat had no lasting repercussions.

9

30

FDR was handsome,
charming, energetic—a
man "breathing health and
virility" in the words of a
military attaché at the
British Embassy. His
infectious high spirits radiate from a photo of him snapped on
a Washington street in July 1920. Women found him immensely attractive, and at parties he was a great flirt. His
relationship with Lucy Mercer (above), Eleanor's social
secretary in Washington, was more than a flirtation, however.
Their attachment strengthened during the long Washington
summers, when Eleanor and the children were away in Campobello. It ended in the summer of 1918, when FDR was faced
with the choice of divorcing Eleanor or breaking off his relationship with Lucy.

Into national politics

Early in his years at the Navy Department, FDR had attempted to run as an anti-Tammany candidate for U.S. Senator from New York. He was badly defeated and the experience taught him a salutary political lesson. Three years later, in July 1917, he made his peace with Tammany's boss, Charles F. Murphy. The way was now prepared for Roosevelt's entry into national politics. In July 1920, FDR was a delegate to the Democratic National Convention in San Francisco. After some wrangling, the convention nominated James Cox, Governor of Ohio, for President. With Tammany's consent, Roosevelt was chosen as the Vice-Presidential nominee.

The 1920 campaign

Cox and Roosevelt decided to make support for the League of Nations the central issue of their campaign. In the White House an invalided President Wilson told them "I am very grateful." FDR campaigned tirelessly. During two days in the State of Washington he managed to give twenty-six speeches. But voters were apathetic about the League, and the Republicans' promise of a "return to normalcy" proved to be irresistible. In the election, Warren G. Harding and his running mate Calvin Coolidge won by a landslide, with some 16 million votes to 9 million for the Democrats. FDR took his defeat with good grace. "Curiously enough," he wrote to a friend three days after the election, "I do not feel in the least bit downhearted."

The polio attack

On 27 July 1921, FDR paid a visit to a Scout Camp at Lake Kanowahke in his capacity as president of the Boy Scout Foundation of Greater New York. A photo taken that day is the last picture of FDR walking unassisted. Two weeks later, at Campobello, he was striken with poliomyelitis. In mid-September he was taken to Presbyterian Hospital in New York City. "I cannot say how long Mr. Roosevelt will be kept in the hospital," his doctor told reporters, "but you can say definitely that he will not be crippled." For years, FDR hopefully believed in the doctor's prediction.

Gradually, FDR came to realize that he would never regain the use of his legs, but he refused to let disability affect his career or his enjoyment of life. Here he is seen sunbathing at Palm Beach with Mrs. Frances de Rham and fishing near Warm Springs, Georgia (one of the rare photos showing his leg braces). The water at Warm Springs did more to alleviate his condition than anything else. FDR invested much of his inheritance in the Georgia Warm Springs Foundation and made regular visits there all his life.

36

Return to politics

37

At the Democratic National Convention in June 1924 (below), FDR nominated Governor Alfred E. Smith of New York for President, calling him "the happy warrior of the political battlefield." However, a deadlock developed at the convention between Smith and William G. McAdoo. In the end, a compromise candidate was selected, John W. Davis. Despite his candidate's defeat, FDR was back in the political limelight. The New York *Herald Tribune* called him "the real hero of the Democratic convention." Masterminding the backstage moves in Roosevelt's reemergence was Louis McHenry Howe (above left), a onetime newspaper reporter who had been his political adviser and manager since 1912. Until his death in 1936, Howe was FDR's closest political mentor and confidant.

38

Governor of New York

he summer of 1928, FDR attended the Democratic National
Convention in Houston as a delegate from New York, and
nce again he made the nominating speech for Al Smith. This
me Smith was chosen as the party's candidate for President.
New York would be an important state in the forthcoming
election, and the Democrats needed a strong candidate to suc-
eed Al Smith as Governor. Rather reluctantly, FDR agreed to
un. In the election, Smith was trounced by Herbert Hoover.
He did not even carry his own State of New York. But
Roosevelt himself squeaked through and won the governor-
hip by the slimmest of margins.

n 1 January 1929 he took office and posed for a ceremonial
hoto with his wife and mother (above). FDR's narrow man-
ate did not make his first term in Albany particularly easy,
ut as Governor of the nation's then most populous state he
ommanded considerable attention.

The Depression

During FDR's second term as Governor of New York, the Depression became ever more severe: national income dropped from $85 to $37 billion, some 5,000 banks closed their doors, unemployment rose to 14 million. Indigent men lived in communities of temporary shacks, known derisively as Hoovervilles. Breadlines proliferated. Worst of all was the feeling of hopelessness that spread across the country. In a speech on 2 May 1932, FDR proclaimed: "The country needs and, unless I mistake its temper, the country demands bold, persistent experimentation. . . . The millions who are in want will not stand by silently forever while the things to satisfy their needs are within easy reach."

The 1932 convention

The day after FDR's reelection as Governor of New York State, Will Rogers commented: "The Democrats nominated their President yesterday." In the event, it didn't happen quite that easily. By early 1932 every pundit and pollster in America was predicting a Democratic landslide later that year, and several contenders began to fancy themselves in the White House. Roosevelt's chief rival was the old "Happy Warrior," Al Smith, who had run unsuccessfully on the Democratic ticket in 1928. The two had for long been close political allies, but in February 1932, Smith announced his availability for the Democratic nomination. On the first roll call at the Democratic convention in July, Roosevelt had 666¼ votes—an impressive tally, but not the two-thirds majority that was then required to win the nomination. On the fourth ballot William G. McAdoo, a victim of the two-thirds majority rule eight years earlier, announced: "California came here to nominate a President of the United States. She did not come to deadlock the convention . . . California casts 44 votes for Franklin D. Roosevelt." That settled it.

FDR broke with tradition by flying out to Chicago to accept his party's nomination in person (below, surrounded by Anna, FDR Jr., James, and—facing camera—Elliott, with campaign manager James A. Farley on the left). To the cheering party faithful at the Chicago Stadium he promised: "I pledge you, I pledge myself, to a new deal for the American people."

The campaign takes off

Although a Democratic victory was virtually assured in the depths of the "Hoover Depression," FDR campaigned vigorously to offset any fears that his disability might impair his performance as President. Right, the traditional whistle-stop greeting at Jefferson City, Missouri. Below, a press conference aboard the campaign train.

43

44

On to Election Day

45

Roosevelt's campaign speeches were deliberately vague. He called for a change of direction but proposed no concrete programs. The campaign was aimed at getting votes, not at defining a new philosophy of government. But there could be no mistaking the candidate's concern for "the forgotten man"— the farmers and workers who had been hardest hit by the Depression. In October 1932 newspaper photographers snapped him greeting farmers in Georgia.

With Eleanor in the back seat of an open touring car, FDR waves to his Hyde Park neighbors on the last night of the campaign. Next day, 8 November 1932, there were smiles of victory at Democratic headquarters in New York's Biltmore Hotel as the returns came in. Roosevelt carried forty-two of the forty-eight states.

46

FDR was the last President-elect obliged to wait four months before taking office. The inauguration would not take place until 4 March 1933. (By an amendment to the Constitution, passed during Herbert Hoover's last days in office, Inauguration Day was moved up to 20 January, beginning in 1937.) During the long interregnum Roosevelt had to sit on the sidelines while the country's economy edged toward complete chaos. Thousands of banks closed their doors to forestall a run on their dwindling liquid assets by anxious depositors, and some never reopened. But without the power to deal effectively with the situation, Roosevelt refused to share responsibility with the "lame duck" occupant of the White House. Everything would have to wait until after March 4.

FDR almost never made it to the White House at all. A few weeks before Inauguration Day, he took a short cruise on Vincent Astor's yacht. Disembarking on 15 February at Miami, the President-elect made a short speech at Bay Front Park, then got back into his car. At that moment a half-crazed bricklayer, Giuseppe Zangara, opened fire. His shots missed Roosevelt but hit several bystanders, including the Mayor of Chicago, Anton Cermak, pictured as he is being helped into Roosevelt's car. FDR visited him next day at Jackson Memorial Hospital. "I'm glad it was me instead of you," Cermak is reported to have said. Three weeks later he was dead.

47

ment of the state-funded Temporary Emergency Relief Administration, or TERA. TERA as the first of the alphabetical agencies Roosevelt was always fond of improvising. Symbolically, it was the first acknowledgment in the United States of the duty of the state and national governments to aid the jobless. (The task had been left to cities, towns, and villages until then. Every New England village had a "poor farm" when I was young.) TERA was also the avenue used by Harry L. Hopkins to enroll in the Roosevelt team. Hopkins, the Iowa harness-maker's son who had become a strange and brilliant amalgam of a do-gooder and racetrack gambler, was recruited into TERA from an important post in privately financed social work in New York City, and he ended as the head of the agency. From this beginning, the later Roosevelt-Hopkins partnership arose.

For Roosevelt's Presidential plans, of course, what happened in New York was important. It would have been harmful if he had so handled the Tammany-Jimmy Walker problem that enemies could seriously accuse him of shoving the problem under the rug to serve his own ambition—a danger which he only barely eluded. It was most helpful to Roosevelt, again, to have gained the name of handling the consequences of the Depression more boldly and humanely than anyone else in a responsible position in those long-gone days.

Yet where the Presidency was concerned, what happened in New York State was very much less important than what was happening in the Democratic Party.

Speaking schematically, what was happening in the Democratic Party was an obscure, unannounced, but still deadly struggle between the people who would become the liberal wing of the Democratic Party—those who rallied around Roosevelt, along with the farmers and some of the Southerners—and the old-style Democratic conservatives of that period, symbolized and largely led by John J. Raskob, the DuPont executive whom Al Smith had installed as chairman of the Democratic National Committee. In order to understand the struggle, you have to imagine an American political spectrum moved far, far to the right of where the spectrum is today.

Raskob's aim was to make the great issue in 1932 the repeal of the Prohibition amendment rather than the Depression. His level of social thought may be judged from the stimulus which later led him to found the Liberty League as an instrument to drive Roosevelt from the White House. The stimulus was an anguished letter from one of the richer members of the DuPont clan, who announced he now knew for certain that the foundations of the Republic were crumbling away, because five black workers on his South Carolina quail plantation had just rejected wages of $1 a day on the shocking ground that they could get a bit more from the Federal government in the form of relief.

Improbable as it may seem nowadays, the struggle with Raskob and his allies was perilous for Roosevelt, Howe, and Farley. Farley's cross-country trips soon revealed that Roosevelt could count with certainty on a substantial majority of the delegates to the Democratic convention in 1932. Yet a substantial majority was not good enough because of the Democratic party's two-thirds rule. With the two-thirds rule still on the books, the Raskob strategy had an excellent chance of success.

Boiled down to essentials, this strategy came in two parts. The first part was to persuade Al Smith to become a candidate again. This would give to Smith—and thus cost Roosevelt—the vote of every delegate Tammany and its friends could still control, which meant a majority of the New York delegates, plus the votes of a good many other delegates controlled by local bosses close to Smith, like Mayor Frank Hague of Jersey City. The strategy's second part was to encourage the maximum number of favorite-son candidacies strong enough to tie up state delegations, and thus to keep these delegations out of the Roosevelt camp. The threat to Roosevelt was serious, too, for he had to gain the two-thirds needed for nomination on a very early ballot of the convention, or else see his own lines break and the convention compromise, as in 1924, on another nominee more acceptable to the minority of the party. If this had happened—and it very nearly did happen—the country would then have had to choose between another four years of Herbert Hoover or a Democratic candidate as wedded to the ways of the American past as Newton D. Baker of Ohio or the Texan Speaker of the House, John Nance Garner. No imagination can compass what the sequels might have been, with one of these past-thinkers in the White House, with the whole economy in collapse, with the unemployment total standing at somewhere between 12 and 14 million (or close to *one-third* of the work force in those days), and with half the farmers and a high percentage of other homeowners in dire danger of having their mortgages foreclosed.

In the circumstances, it is understandable that Roosevelt's pre-convention effort was to round up as many committed delegates as he could, to sound no alarmingly new or controversial notes, and to placate all power centers capable of being placated. Incredible as it now seems, Roosevelt's most important act of placation was an announcement that he no longer favored American entry into the League of Nations. This was aimed to soothe the suspicions of the megalomaniac isolationist William Randolph Hearst. Later, Hearst died on the naked brink of bankruptcy because he never understood either the impact on the mass readership of his newspapers of Roosevelt and the New Deal, or the impact on his personal affairs of the new level of federal income taxation. But in 1930–32, Hearst was still a commandingly powerful man. He was largely responsible for John Nance Garner's favorite-son candidacy in Texas, and almost solely responsible for the votes of the large California delegation to the Democratic convention going to Garner in 1932. Roosevelt's statement on the League of Nations by no means brought Hearst into the Roosevelt camp, but at least it convinced Hearst that Roosevelt was no longer a "Wilsonian internationalist" who must be fought to the death and at all costs.

Once Raskob and his allies had played upon Smith's increasing bitterness towards Roosevelt until he agreed to become a candidate—which took some time—all the pieces of the stop-Roosevelt strategy were in place and in working order. Hence the Democrats' 1932 convention was one of the most exciting in the nation's political history, but it will be enough here to set down the salient facts. The site of the convention was Chicago, which was an advantage for the stop-Roosevelt people. These ranged through the whole spectrum, including the disheveled populist Governor of Oklahoma, "Alfalfa Bill" Murray; but the key man was Al Smith, at least for the early ballots, and Chicago was Smith territory. This was because Smith's most lasting contribution to the Democratic Party had been in 1928, when he managed to interest the mass voters in the big cities for the first time in national politics as well as city politics.

Roosevelt had also made the pre-convention error of challenging Smith in Massachusetts, where the Democratic

Party was then close to being an Irish Roman Catholic party. Smith in consequence had not only won in Massachusetts by a large majority, but had also rounded up most of the other New England delgates. The New Englanders plus his other supporters gave Smith more than 200 votes in all. The favorite sons—Garner, Murray, and others too obscure to be worth listing—had enough additional first-ballot votes to keep the Roosevelt first-ballot total to 650 votes-plus. This amounted to a comfortable majority of the national convention but sadly far from a two-thirds majority.

After that, the only question was where the first break would come and who would be favored when it did. From the start until close to the finish, it appeared most likely that the Roosevelt lines would break first. Mathematically, this was the result to expect, for Roosevelt not only had much the largest number of delegates; in addition, many of his delegations were far from closely controlled. The Mississippi delegation nearly did break away, but was herded back into the Roosevelt lines by the impassioned exhortations of Huey Long of Louisiana, who was a strong Roosevelt backer in 1932 and then became Roosevelt's most feared political enemy in the Democratic Party until he was assassinated.

Roosevelt, who was watching developments from the Governor's mansion in Albany, and Farley and Howe in Chicago all perceived that their best chance was offered by the large bloc of Texas and California votes pledged to Speaker of the House Garner. Just how the thing was done is not quite clear to this day. But it is certain that Hearst, who largely controlled California, was persuaded that if Roosevelt failed, the convention would end by choosing the arch-"Wilsonian internationalist" Newton D. Baker. This made Roosevelt the lesser evil, and Hearst therefore agreed to give the Californians the signal for Roosevelt if Garner did not object.

It is also certain that Garner did not want the Vice Presidency, rightly considering the Speakership of the House a far more important position. But Garner was both a deeply loyal Democrat and a splendidly patriotic American who feared what would happen to the country he loved if the quarrels of the Democrats gave Herbert Hoover another real chance at the White House. The upshot was that Garner agreed to accept second place on the ticket and California and Texas went for Roosevelt on the fourth ballot, just in time to prevent the first serious vote losses which always spell the doom of a front-running candidate. William Gibbs McAdoo revenged himself on Al Smith for what had happened in 1924 by announcing California's change of heart early in the roll call. Everyone could then see what was sure to happen, and the ensuing stampede to Roosevelt was so rapid that the Texas votes hardly counted when they were added to the Roosevelt total.

The only flaw was that Smith refused to make the party nominations unanimous and left Chicago in a fury. But that hardly mattered. Roosevelt, as soon as he got the results in Albany, ordered a plane to carry him, his wife, and some other members of his family and staff to Chicago, where he meant to deliver his acceptance speech to the convention in person. This was—again it seems almost incredible—a bold break with political tradition, for under existing rules (which had been laid down in the era before there were even telegraph wires) successful candidates always stayed demurely at home until formally "notified" that they had won the party nomination. They then delivered their "acceptance" speeches from their front porches or the equivalent.

While waiting for the nominee, the convention occupied itself with nominating Garner for the Vice Presidency. The delegates had a long wait, for the aircraft Roosevelt had chartered was small and slow. The weather was also bad, and the flight from Albany to Chicago took many hours and would probably have congealed with alarm the most hardened fliers of today. Roosevelt was cheerfully immune to physical fear in any form, however; so he spent the time in the air happily working on his acceptance speech, and finally emerged from the plane in Chicago as fit as a fiddle and wreathed in smiles. Well he might smile, too, for this was the end of the beginning, which had come just as he had hoped it would come when he gave Grenville Clark his plans for reaching the Presidency before he first ran for the New York State Senate more than twenty years earlier.

The national campaign that followed has always been a main count against Roosevelt among the sect of academic theorists who now tend to downgrade Roosevelt's achievement, on the ground that he did not effect the kind of revolutionary transformation of the entire American polity which he would have been the first to oppose. These people are too remote from any recognizable reality to understand Rule I of leadership, which Roosevelt understood thoroughly. Rule I, at any rate in America, is that you have to be a good politician in order to get the chance to be a great statesman. And from the standpoint of Rule I, the campaign Roosevelt waged in 1932 deserves to be included as a model in every primer for aspiring American leaders.

There are two things to remember about the situation in 1932 if you wish to understand the campaign. The first is that Herbert Hoover had already done most of Roosevelt's work for him, for by that year the glum "free enterprise" doctrinaire in the White House had alienated most of the major groups in the American electorate, including large sectors of the middle and business classes. Hoover had no hope at all except from the fact that the Republicans then commanded a natural electoral majority. The trick for Roosevelt was not to drive the discontented Republicans back to their own party, either by waging the kind of empty, nothing-campaign that lost the election for Thomas E. Dewey in 1948 or, worse still, by appearing to be what would have been regarded as a left-wing extremist by the peculiar standards of that period.

Roosevelt avoided the Dewey pitfall by pouring out his limitless energy in appearances all over the United States, by exerting his charm and exhibiting his buoyancy at every whistle-stop, and by making a great number of speeches which aroused hope without arousing opposition.

As for the "extremist" pitfall, Roosevelt avoided this with even greater ease, because he was not an extremist and never became one. Nowadays, his most criticized speech of the whole campaign is the one he gave late in the campaign in Pittsburgh, where he denounced Hoover for failing to balance the federal budget. But the truth is, Roosevelt firmly believed in balanced budgets in 1932, as he later showed by naming Lewis W. Douglas his Budget Director after his inauguration, and then backing Lew Douglas in a series of severe budget cuts. Poor Hoover, meanwhile, could hardly show himself on the streets without being booed, and in all his speeches he divided his time between prosily defending his own record and emitting anguished warnings about the dire consequences to be expected from the election of his opponent. The result, inevitably, was the first Roosevelt landslide.

Thereafter there was an interval of four long months before the inauguration, for though new Presidents were then chosen early in November as they are today, they took office only the next March. The long interval was a hair-raising period, although useful to Roosevelt in the sense that it gave him plenty of time to choose his Cabinet and the personal advisers he wished to take to Washington. These months set the stage for the drama of the inauguration in a quite different way, however. The economy, which had shown faint signs of incipient recovery earlier in the year, went into another slump in the autumn. Even more men were added to the rolls of the millions of jobless, and this time the banks began to crack *en masse* during the winter. Michigan was the first state to declare a bank holiday, but one by one a long list of other states had to follow Michigan's example.

President Hoover desperately and repeatedly offered "cooperation" to his successor, and then blamed Roosevelt for refusing to "cooperate." But what Hoover really offered was a chance for his successor to commit himself irrevocably to Hoover's principles and a Hoover-style economic approach. This all came to an end when Roosevelt took the oath of office on the family Bible, on that fear-ridden day when the last solvent banks in the nation were being driven to close and some sort of end of the road seemed to have been reached by the United States.

Before placing Roosevelt on the platform built out from the Capitol steps, where Chief Justice Charles Evan Hughes administered the oath to him, two short detours are desirable to deal with two questions of enduring importance in the new President's life and career in the White House.

The first is how matters had gone between him and his wife after that day in 1918 when she had come upon Lucy Mercer's letters to him. From that day forward, as I have already suggested, the evidence—what there is of it—suggests that Franklin and Eleanor Roosevelt became highly successful working partners rather than a married couple of the usual sort. If there were other women—and again the evidence suggests there were in the long interval before the Second World War—their identities have never been established with certainty. But the change went much further than that, for Eleanor Roosevelt emancipated herself in a truly remarkable way. When the early Washington years were over, she found a place for herself in the women's activities of the Democratic Party; and this work occupied her fully when she was not accompanying her husband on his barnstorming trips in the 1920 campaign. Later, she took a regular job teaching three days a week at the Todhunter School for girls in New York City.

The days of meek submissiveness to Mrs. James Roosevelt were over, and Eleanor Roosevelt eventually moved out of the Hyde Park house for good, to all intents, when she built herself a cottage on the property. She shared this house with Miss Marion Dickerman and Miss Nancy Cook; there were other women friends in New York City as well; and in the end there was Lorena Hickok, the Associated Press correspondent assigned to cover the manifold activities of the candidate's wife when Roosevelt began to seek the Presidency openly. Miss Hickok undoubtedly fell deeply in love with the heroine of her news stories.

There is no use pretending that the atmosphere Eleanor Roosevelt lived in during the Twenties and the early Thirties was not a partly Lesbian atmosphere, or blinking the fact that a substantial share of her women friends away from Hyde Park were consciously or unconsciously Lesbians, or denying that Eleanor Roosevelt herself distinctly admired the independence of these other women on their own and even much enjoyed the gush and admiration some of them gave to her. It is unthinkable to me, however, as it is to every other person known to me who was fairly close to Eleanor Roosevelt, that she ever went, or was even tempted to go, a particle further than accepting gush and admiration and sometimes repaying the debt in the same coin, as in the letters now deposited at Hyde Park as a result of Lorena Hickok's recent death. Perhaps it would have been better for her if she had done differently, for she was plainly a woman richly capable of love. But I do not believe she *could* have done differently because of the strength of her character and her training.

Meanwhile, and infinitely more important, Eleanor Roosevelt in her new independence helped Franklin Roosevelt far more than she ever had when she was trying her best to be a conventional wife and mother. Perhaps her most important contribution in this first phase was to make her husband aware of the political potential of the other half of the human race. He and she together helped her friend, the vigorous Molly Dewson, to carve out a whole female empire for herself in the New York State Democratic organization. Then, too, Eleanor Roosevelt gradually persuaded her husband that women needed fuller recognition, primarily in the form of appointments to responsible jobs in government, in order to bring these newly enfranchised voters into

72

the political process in earnest. She created the climate, in truth, in which Roosevelt first made Frances Perkins Commissioner of Labor in New York, and then brought her to Washington to become the most distinguished Secretary of Labor the U.S. Government has ever had.

Through Eleanor Roosevelt's determined good offices, her husband also made contact for the first time with a whole series of spheres that had been unknown to him—of the social workers and other reformers, of the more intellectual labor leaders like David Dubinsky and Sidney Hillman, and of all sorts of other people with ideas socially advanced by the standards of that period. All of this was invaluable preparation for Roosevelt, for it played a large part in stretching his mind, so to say, to the point that he was mentally flexible enough for the fearful task awaiting him when he won the Presidency. Nor was that all. Because of his disability, he could never really go and see for himself. So his wife learned to be his eyes and ears in all sorts of situations which were physically inaccessible to him. And all this must be understood by anyone who wishes to understand the White House years; for the Eleanor Roosevelt of those years was simply a mature magnification of the Eleanor Roosevelt who declared her independence in 1920.

The other question that needs to be considered, if the White House years are to be comprehensible, is the most difficult of all the questions this memoir must confront. Just what sort of man was the Franklin Roosevelt who told the paralyzed country on his inauguration day, "The only thing to fear is fear itself"? One of his closest friends, the already cited William Phillips, once said that this question could not be answered because Roosevelt was three or four different men, and one never could tell in advance which of these *personae* would be sitting in the President's chair on any given occasion. It seems to me that this was a true verdict. Yet in some sense it was also an irrelevant verdict, for what one really wants to know about are the qualities which made him a great statesman, as I believe he was after he became President and whenever the need for statesmanship arose. This is the puzzle I must now tackle, for thus far I have all but exclusively investigated the qualities that made Roosevelt a superlative political leader.

To begin with the positive negatives, as one may call them, Franklin D. Roosevelt was not an ideologist, or a

73

theory-monger, or a man with a gospel to peddle. If he dismissed an argument on the ground that "it's all very theoretical," that was a final dismissal. He disliked and distrusted ideologists, whether of the right or the left. Results were his only tests where political action was under consideration.

Roosevelt's total preoccupation with results in turn explains some of the things he did not do that many now think he ought to have done—most notably in the area of civil rights. Certainly, the Roosevelt relief and other social programs were color-blind in a way that was genuinely novel in the U.S. government in those days, as can be deduced from the anguished shock of the member of the DuPont clan already mentioned. Few men have had more political foresight than Roosevelt, and he must have foreseen quite clearly that when he and his wife managed to make Democrats of almost all voting blacks, the end result could only be to give the black voters great leverage with the Democratic Party, at least in the North—which duly happened with far-reaching consequences.

Yet his preoccupation with results still limited Roosevelt's own overt civil rights action to a flannelly stand in favor of an anti-lynching bill. The main obstacles to bolder action were two. On the one hand, the country's white majority in the 1930s would not have tolerated the kind of civil rights movement which commanded such strong support in the 1960s. On the other hand, Roosevelt's famous New Deal coalition comprised three very disparate partners: the traditional Democrats of the South, the big-city bosses, and labor union members and the rest of the great mass of poorer people in the North. Furthermore, the Southerners had a whiphand of sorts, simply because the senior Congressional Democrats, who led the party in the House and Senate and occupied the key committee chairmanships, were Southerners with few exceptions.

If Roosevelt had gone all-out for civl rights, he would have been most unlikely to succeed, and he would surely have lost the chance to do most of the rest of the good things he did. That is why he did not go all-out. Moreover, this is only one of the reasons you cannot comprehend Franklin Roosevelt's mode of operation, and even admire his remarkable record, if you cannot sympathize with his oft-repeated, half humorous plaint (often about his wife): "Some people can never understand that you have to wait, even for the best things, until the right time comes."

So much for what I have called the positive negatives of Roosevelt as a leader. In addition, there were unqualified positives to constitute the other side of the medal. The first of the positives was Roosevelt's pragmatism. Being anti-ideological, he did not suffer from that great enemy of statesmanship, the disease of rigid adherence to a theoretically developed plan of action. He had goals, great goals, as statesmen must. But the goal was what he cared about, and not how he got there. If one device failed him, he was perfectly ready to try another device for reaching a major goal. So he reached a surprising number of his goals in the end, although not without zigzags which bewildered, even horrified, a great many worthy people.

The plain truth is that Roosevelt was perfectly ready to follow a political course that would have broken a snake's back if that course finally took him to where he wanted to be. Thus we shall find that the first New Deal, in the years 1933 and 1934, was markedly different in the character of its measures and its underlying thought from the second New Deal of the years 1935 and 1936; that the next period, roughly 1937 and 1938, was again different and much more strident and contentious; and that in late 1938 Roosevelt fairly abruptly turned his back on all domestic concerns in order to cope with the ever-growing dangers of the world situation. This sort of thing, plus Roosevelt's pragmatism and abhorrence of theory, in combination explain the poor impression he tended to make on higher thinkers.

After a meeting at the White House, John Maynard Keynes patronizingly remarked that Roosevelt really seemed to know nothing of economic theory. Of the same order was the equally patronizing summation of the new President by Justice Oliver Wendell Holmes, after Roosevelt had taken great trouble to pay Holmes a ceremonial visit when the great Justice was past ninety. Roosevelt, said Holmes, had no better than a second-class mind—although Holmes granted him a "first-class temperament." And of course Roosevelt could never imaginably have elaborated Keynes's economic doctrines, any more than he could have written one of Justice Holmes's magnificent philosophical dissents. He was not an intellectual, even in the sense that the hero of his young years, Theodore Roosevelt, had been an intellectual. Yet all that he did—all that made him one of the great Presidents—could never have been done by Holmes, or by an American Keynes, or by Edmund Wilson, or by any of the other intellectuals who either spoke patronizingly of him or like Wilson held him in open detestation. The doing began, too, the day Roosevelt was inaugurated in Washington.

THE NEW DEAL

A cold-blooded and knowledgeable observer, watching the beginning of the first Roosevelt administration that frightening March day long ago, would have been justified in refusing to offer a boundlessly optimistic long-range forecast. The first inaugural address was delivered when total ruin seemed to stare the nation in the face; and it gave the entire nation new hope—but mainly because the new President was so glowingly hopeful and confident himself.

Certainly, the Cabinet which Roosevelt brought to Washington was by no means an undiluted assemblage of first-class men. The Secretary of State, Cordell Hull, was a splendid old Tennessee mountaineer with an obsession about free trade; the Secretary of the Treasury, William Woodin, an intelligent, kindly but rather wispy industrialist. The other Cabinet members deserving mention were the politically wise and useful Jim Farley, who was Postmaster General; the Secretary of Agriculture, Henry A. Wallace, a man immensely knowledgeable about farm problems but a mystic and an unreliable oddity when too far from the furrow and the manure pile; the Secretary of Labor, Frances Perkins, longest enduring of the lot by reason of superior human quality; and the able and combative Secretary of the Interior, Harold L. Ickes. For the rest, none needs to be mentioned except for the Secretary of the Navy, Claude Swanson, who was only memorable for two quite extraneous reasons. His partner in Virginia politics had been the most curiously named of all American politicians, C. Bascom Slemp, universally known as "the sly Slemp." And Swanson was the man who laid down the first law of politics, "When the water reaches the upper deck, follow the rats!"

Roosevelt's close friend and Hyde Park neighbor Henry Morgenthau, Jr. came to Washington with him, and after heading the Farm Credit Administration for a while, became Secretary of the Treasury when Woodin succumbed to cancer. Then there were the intellectuals-turned-Presidential advisers from the pre-convention and campaign teams, most notably Raymond Moley, Rexford G. Tugwell, and Adolf A. Berle, Jr. In the long pull, these men were mainly important as presages of the others of fairly similar origins who came later and gave the peacetime New Deal its strongest human flavor. For a time, however, the first-comers were also important in themselves, and especially so in the cases of Moley and Tugwell.

Moley was a marvelous speech writer, fertile in ideas, then thought to be far to the left, but in fact strongly pro-business. Tugwell was a handsome, vain man—he usually wore a blue shirt the exact color of his eyes—and he was a genuine left-winger in the old-fashioned do-good style with up-to-date intellectual overtones. Both Moley and Tugwell were economic nationalists, and both came close to believing in the doctrines of state planning and autarchy that were modishly peddled at that period. Neither lasted very long, Moley because he got too big for his boots and underrated the Tennessee mountaineer's feuding skill of his official chief, Cordell Hull, and Tugwell because his sense of political realities was deficient and he was hardly worth the controversy he evoked.

Furthermore, neither the first New Dealers, nor the members of the Cabinet, nor even the President himself (one may guess) had a very clear idea of what should be done immediately about the total collapse of the credit machinery of the country because of the failure of the banking system. The Emergency Banking Relief Act and the proclamation of a national bank holiday were largely the work of Hoover hold-overs: the extremely able but high-Tory former Secretary of the Treasury, Ogden L. Mills, and Mills's former subordinate at the Treasury, Arthur Ballantine. Both of them stayed on to work around the clock with Secretary of the Treasury Woodin until the Emergency Banking Relief Act could be sent up to the Congress. There was only one copy, which was read to the House of Representatives while the bill itself, as formally introduced, was just a roll of newspapers. None the less, the recognition of the emergency was so universal, and the new climate Roosevelt's pesonality had already generated was so strong, that the House passed the roll of newspapers without audible argument and all but instantaneously. The country also accepted the bank holiday as something close to a general holiday—at any rate for those who were not in the tragic ranks of the unemployed—and the change of climate was then proved all over again when the more solvent banks nervously reopened at last, and money flowed back into them from all sorts of people who had been desperate to get their deposits out when the banks were closing on all sides. Yet that first surge of hope was no instant cure of the grim ills of the times.

Anecdotal evidence, I know, is always to be distrusted, yet I cannot help feeling that the hardly imaginable flavor of that time is best conveyed by personal experience. In brief, I went to work in New York on the *Herald Tribune* on 5 July 1932, at $20 a week. This was reduced the next week to $18 by a 10 per cent paycut for all—and at that I was lucky to have the job. I was also particularly lucky in having a tiny income of my own. My oldest friend, Bill Patten, had similarly modest revenues; yet we could comfortably afford a pleasant walk-up apartment on Manhattan's East Side (two bedroooms, large sitting room, large kitchen, and bath for $60 a month), plus a man to clean and cook for us, do our washing, press our suits, and shine our shoes.

I still recall with guilt that the first man was a Puerto Rican, who begged for the job and promised to do it all for $7 a week. It was hopeless, for he spoke almost no English and had not the faintest idea of what he was supposed to do, so we got a Japanese-American who performed all the same tasks ideally for several years on end, and for $15 a week. I further remember with deep shame how the Puerto Rican wept when we told him we could not keep him, and the shame is not much reduced by the fact that Bill Patten and I gave him every cent we could lay our hands on except subway fare to our respective jobs, causing him to bless us profusely as he returned to joblessness! With even deeper horror, however, I recall occasional taxi rides down what has now become Franklin Delano Roosevelt Drive, to see my grandmother when she was lying ill in her New York house. Manhattan's East River waterfront, in those days, was where the mountainous city dumps were located; and there were always people, mostly respectable-looking older men and women, climbing precariously about on the enormous dumps in the hope of finding bits of edible garbage! *That* was the state of the nation months after Roosevelt took over the leadership—and things were of course much worse in other localities than they were in New York.

This situation was only slowly altered. There was a tolerated "Hooverville" of homeless men living in shacks in the middle of Central Park throughout most of 1933; hence it may be wondered how Roosevelt managed to maintain the climate of hope so magically restored by his inaugural. The answer is that he never gave the country time to lose hope until much later in the game, and instead of withdrawing into the shadows of the White House, as Hoover had so often done, he never left the forefront of the action, where he orchestrated the growth of hope in the fullest possible limelight. The action was breathtaking for a considerable period, too, for he first called on Congress to remain in Washington in continuous emergency session, to receive and act upon an unceasing succession of bills he sent up to the Hill; and when the "Hundred Days" were over, his proposals to Congress continued thick and fast into 1934. In this memoir, however, there is no place for a detailed historical account of the First New Deal, as this period came to be called later. I shall content myself with grouping the main actions Roosevelt took, according to my notion of their permanent significance.

First, in my judgment, must come the measures and agencies that started America down the road leading to our version of the welfare state. Of these agencies, two undertook specific tasks that the Federal government is still performing. The Farm Credit Administration, initially under Henry Morgenthau, ended by refinancing no less than one-fifth of all the farm mortgages in the country. And the Home Owners' Loan Corporation achieved a similar record with private urban and suburban mortgages.

Even more important, however, was the first agency aimed to provide more generous relief for the plight of the jobless. The Federal Emergency Relief Administration was authorized to give direct cash grants to the states, and thus to pay the states for their relief payments to their citizens in need. FERA was given an appropriation of $500 million and Harry Hopkins was called to Washington to spend the money. Hopkins dispersed funds so rapidly that the *Washington Post* carried the worried headline, MONEY FLIES, only twenty-four hours after he first set up shop in the lobby of a building used for other purposes.

To complete the story, FERA was replaced, when the money ran out, with the Civil Works Agency, with a much larger appropriation which Hopkins spent on directly provided Federal Work Relief. The newspapers labeled it "leaf-raking," and some of it was just that although most was not; but this did not matter to Hopkins, for the money was going to hungry people without other resources. "Hunger is not debatable," was one of Hopkins's mottoes of this early time; and it led on eventually to the largest of his relief programs, the Works Progress Administration. Even the WPA has long belonged to history, although millions were on its rolls for a period of years. But the effect of these Hopkins-guided relief programs is still with us, for they firmly established the principle of federal responsibility to aid the jobless and destitute; and the principle then gave birth to the unemployment benefits included in the Social Security System, and to the welfare programs of the Department of Health and Welfare.

Next in importance, because they also lasted in one way or another, was a series of diverse measures on a number of quite different fronts, passed at different times during the two years of the First New Deal. For two of these measures only limited credit can be given to Roosevelt, for they originated elsewhere. The true-blue Republican Senator Arthur H. Vandenberg of Michigan was the real author of Federal Deposit Insurance for banks. Roosevelt opposed the plan because he thought it would not work, but he reluctantly signed the bill when it passed Congress, and Vandenberg's scheme has been working admirably ever since.

More moving and instructive, however—for it concerns a great old hero and reveals a major unnoticed change in American policy-making—is the story behind the Tennessee Valley Authority. As to the unnoticed change, until the Second World War the liberals and progressives in Congress were by no means content simply to make noble speeches, strike noble attitudes, and cast noble votes. Since 1945, no single major piece of forward-looking legislation which finally reached the statute books has been owed, individually, to one of the Senators or Representatives from the left side of the political spectrum. In the earlier time, however, the able men on the left side of the spectrum, particularly Senators, used to make specialties of this great problem or that, to develop their own solutions, and to fight for them year after year until their solutions became the law of the land when the time was ripe. Preeminent among these true lawmakers of the past was Senator George W. Norris of Nebraska, one of the most admirable figures I have known in American public life. All through the 1920s, Norris had fought off grabs by the private power interests for the great government-built power dam at Muscle Shoals dating from the First World War, and in the course of these fights Norris had developed the main outlines of the plan for the Tennessee Valley Authority. Roosevelt, who revered Norris, strongly supported the TVA, and so the Norris plan, as somewhat amplified by Roosevelt and his advisers, was enacted by Congress with results the world still envies and admires.

Roosevelt himself at first acted on the economic front in a manner a little reminiscent of Alice with the pills and small cakes, which either made her shoot up to giant size or shrink to a midget. In the first fervor of the Hundred Days he secured unprecedented blanket authority for himself and his chosen Budget Director to cut all federal expenditures with complete ruthlessness in order to balance the budget. Budget Director Lewis W. Douglas went to work with a will, making heavy cuts everywhere, including the previously sacred expenditures for war veterans. The result, of course, was harshly deflationary. But after some time had passed, Roosevelt briskly balanced off Douglas's budget-balancing by taking the opposite tack. The International Economic Conference in London had been planned as a meeting to secure economic stabilization, including monetary stabilization. Somewhat belatedly and with an insouciance that still seems a bit shocking, Roosevelt torpedoed the conference in London, and a bit later he unhooked the dollar from gold. Thus Roosevelt contrived what amounted to a *re*flationary devaluation of the dollar, which went by stages until he decided to stabilize again with gold at a new value of $35 an ounce.

These last events are worth noting for another reason, because they led to the first major human casualties of Roosevelt's Presidency. With great drama, Raymond Moley had been added to the U.S. delegation to the London conference with an ill-defined special mission; he had swelled about London in a highly conspicuous way; and then, when he tried to take independent action, he had been stingingly rebuked by the President. Worse still, Moley had given bitter offence in London to Cordell Hull, who therefore set out in earnest to get the Moley-coonskin on his door, and got it before long. When he was riding high, Moley had been described rather regularly as "the assistant President," but he was also the first man whom Roosevelt discarded like a skimmed morning paper. Then the gold decision led the brilliant but erratic New York banker James Warburg to leave the administration. Dean G. Acheson, who opposed the gold decision, was quite groundlessly suspected of disloyalty by Roosevelt and was dismissed from his post in the Treasury. Meanwhile, however, clever young men were already pouring into Washington en masse, all looking for posts in the New Deal, and Felix Frankfurter at Harvard Law School was already serving as the New Deal's chief high-level recruiting officer.

This is far from the whole story. Completeness would make the list of major legislation during the First New Deal altogether too long, but there are certain other measures of several sorts which require to be listed because their effects are still with us in one way or another. Regulation of the securities markets began very early with the first of the Roosevelt Securities Acts, which gave the Federal Trade Commission the task of preventing the more outrageous stock-peddling practices of the years of the false boom. Early on, too, Roosevelt sponsored and pushed through the legislation setting up the Public Works Administration and his special personal project, the Civilian Conservation Corps. Under the suspicious, puritanically honest, and pugnacious old Theodore Roosevelt-Progressive, Secretary Ickes of the Interior Department, public works proceeded slowly and were much criticized for so doing; yet we owe to the PWA the Triborough Bridge in New York City, the port of Brownsville in Texas, countless other structures of nearly comparable importance, all sorts of public buildings, including tens of thousands of county courthouses, and God knows how many other still-useful public works. As for the Civilian Conservation Corps, its 500,000 previously unemployed young men planted more trees than have ever been planted in the United States before or since by private and governmental action combined.

Finally, soil conservation work also began early at the Agriculture Department under the auspices of Henry Wallace, and contour ploughing and many other practices now taken for granted were thus first introduced to American

82

agriculture. But the great era of soil conservation only came later, when drought and wind seared the Great Plains; the whole country was appalled by the appearance of the Dust Bowl with all its awful human consequences, and Roosevelt not only put soil conservation into high gear with an organization solely charged with the task, but also personally pushed through the widely mocked scheme for shelter belts of trees, which admirably protected the Dust Bowl area from wind erosion despite the mockers.

Last of all in this review of the measures of the First New Deal must come the two great measures which made the most noise, stirred up the most excitement at the time, and left the fewest traces behind them. The first Agricultural Adjustment Act was a mish-mash, for Roosevelt chose to elude the programmatic battles among the various farm organizations by putting all their conflicting programs into a single bill and authorizing the lot. None the less, the Agricultural Adjustment Administration got a lot of money to the farmers, who needed it badly, albeit without really tackling the grave problem of agricultural surpluses.

As for the National Recovery Administration, nothing attracted so much attention in the earliest period of the New Deal as the NRA, with its blue eagle, its codes for countless businesses and industries, little and big, and its general atmosphere of an economic camp meeting. It was supposed to promote recovery, and it did some good for a while, although most of the "confidence" it generated derived from the openings provided for price-fixing by businessmen in the different businesses and industries. The NRA codes also effectively ended child labor in the United States and made one or two other lesser advances of that kind, but it was an ill-conceived monster all the same. All things being equal and in the light of hindsight, Roosevelt should have been grateful when the Supreme Court finally struck down first NRA and then AAA. He was anything but grateful, but by the time they were condemned as unconstitutional, both had outlived their usefulness in different ways.

Such was the First New Deal. What very few people understand, even today, is that the First New Deal by no means directly led the way to the Second New Deal. A series of steps of enduring importance were taken by Roosevelt in his first two years in office, as the foregoing pages should be enough to indicate; yet the aims, the dominant ideas, and the persons generating dominant ideas all changed fairly radically when the first two years were over. The simplest test is the fact that TVA was the only creation of the First New Deal which was welcomed with genuine enthusiasm by Justice Louis Dembitz Brandeis, the great philosophical enemy of business bigness. The truth is that despite the social activism and the fruitfulness of individual innovating measures, the First New Deal never tackled the fundamental problem of the relationship between government and business. From the moment when really big business emerged in the United States after the Civil War, big business had always had more to say about national policy than the government itself, barring the special interludes of the Theodore Roosevelt and first Wilson administrations. Nor did this disturb the President's chief advisers of the First New Deal period.

Moley and Tugwell were economic nationalists and believers in planning who thought Justice Brandeis's distaste for business bigness sadly old hat. (They also thought Cordell Hull was sadly old hat in his passion for freer international trade, and although Hull was given his Trade Agreements Act in 1934, it was almost like giving a child a toy, for no one then expected Hull to achieve much with the new law.) Moley was strongly pro-business at heart, as I have said. To head the NRA and AAA, Roosevelt further took General Hugh S. Johnson and George Peek straight out of Bernard M. Baruch's stable, and when General Johnson fell by the wayside he was replaced with the equally business-minded Donald Richberg.

One should not forget, either, the man Roosevelt brought to Washington to give a new direction to the Hoover-era Reconstruction Finance Corporation, the very big businessman from Texas, Jesse Jones. Jones was always a bit of a loner in government, but he was certainly one of the ablest men Roosevelt ever recruited; he loved power; and he used the RFC to promote recovery in a bold new way that gave him authority, for a while, which ramified into most areas of the American corporate world. Not at all incidentally, he also launched a series of subsidiary organizations of lasting import: the federal mortgage agencies, the Commodity Credit Corporation, the Electric Home and Farm Authority, and the Export-Import Bank. Like most rich Texans, Jones mingled distrust for the main financial centers of the Northeast with a certain contempt for them; but his mere presence in Washington was always reassuring to businessmen everywhere.

None the less, the first grave fissures in the relationship between Roosevelt and the businessmen were clearly visible before the First New Deal ended. The biggest fissure of all the early ones was caused by the bill setting up the Securities and Exchange Commission. Some such legislation was unavoidable, after the unceasing revelations of scandals in the financial world by the various investigations then going on in Congress. Study the testimony on the new bill by the president of the New York Stock Exchange, Richard Whitney, however. You will see that the scandals (soon to be supplemented by Whitney himself) meant literally nothing to the more arrogant business leaders, and that such men would have been satisfied with nothing less than Roosevelt deferring to them with humble respect on all questions.

Then, too, the businessmen were more and more outraged by the increasing budget deficits to which Lew Douglas's balanced budget had unavoidably given way because of relief and other urgent expenditures; and there were the other provocations like the one which so upset the member of the DuPont clan who wrote the letter to Raskob. The letter was in fact written, and the Liberty League was flamboyantly founded, in the course of 1934. All the same, Roosevelt clung to what he called "evenhandedness" through most of that year. In March he went so far as proposing that the Democrats' chief fund-raising rallies, the Jefferson Day dinners, be transformed into nonpartisan celebrations with places for Republican businessmen on an equality with people who had always been Democrats. Before the 1934 election, too, Raymond Moley was not wholly repudiated when he blandly announced that the very last unsettling New Deal measure had already passed into law, and tranquility lay just around the corner.

Yet by the end of 1934, it was already plain that the President could no longer shirk the choice which would lead to what I consider one of the greatest Roosevelt achievements. This was bringing the relationship between government and business into a better balance, so that the nation's elected government thereafter called the tune on national policy for good or ill.

The choice could not be shirked, first of all, because the effect of the mounting business hostility to Roosevelt had been strongly reinforced by pressure from the grass roots. After supporting Roosevelt in 1932, Huey Long of Louisiana

(whom Roosevelt regarded as one of the "two most dangerous men in America," the other being General Douglas
MacArthur) had soon quarreled with the President. This
meant that Long's private but impressively strong ultra-
populist movement, with its slogan "Every Man a King,"
was quite likely to turn into an extremely threatening third
party movement in 1936. In September 1935, Long was assassinated by an obscure young man called Weiss who
feared the Fascist tendency of the political dictator of Louisiana; but while he lasted, the threat he posed was real. To
make it worse, Long had showed signs of making alliances
with amiable, bewildered old Dr. Francis Townsend, whose
home-made pension plan had much appeal to old people, and
with the priestly radio-demagogue Father Charles Coughlin.
Coughlin too had turned against Roosevelt, and his radio
audience was said to be the largest ever known.

In addition, as soon as the situation in the country began
to get a bit better, one natural effect of this was to give
people the energy and courage to manifest the discontent
they had been too hopeless to manifest before. In the farming areas, particularly, there were strikes of several sorts
which led to serious disorder; mortgages were burnt; angry
crowds prevented foreclosure sales of farms; and, more than
once, judges authorizing mortgage foreclosures were men-
aced with lynching. In 1934, moreover, when the Republicans would normally have regained a little strength in Congress in the off-year, the Democrats instead made significant
gains. Thus both House and Senate moved noticeably to the
left, and the new balance on Capitol Hill was still another
fact the pragmatist Roosevelt had to take into account.

The President's response was the Second New Deal,
which entirely satisfied Justice Brandeis, not just because
the measures were different, but also because the men who
devised the measures were different. Roosevelt's advisers of
the period of the First New Deal—those of them who had
lasted so long—now began to fade away or even to resign in
protest, as Lew Douglas did. The true New Dealers—or so I
consider them, for I believe they did a far better, more
thoughtful and practical job for their President than their
predecessors had done—now took over in full force. These
were the younger men, often lawyers, and often recruited by
Felix Frankfurter, who were typified by that outwardly ill-
assorted team, Benjamin V. Cohen, the lawyer-thinker with
the exterior of a great Talmudic scholar, and Thomas G.

86

Corcoran, the doer with the exterior of a pious choir boy in an Irish Catholic Church (which in fact he had been before becoming a brilliant graduate of Harvard Law School and Justice Holmes's most famous law clerk). Corcoran and Cohen were probably the best draftsmen of great and complex pieces of legislation Washington has ever seen. But they were something better than that too.

Cohen was a superb legislative strategist, and Corcoran had the down-to-earth understanding of a superlative lobbyist (he later became one) who knew all the ins and outs of passing difficult bills through Congress. Nor were they without ideas of their own, and thus they were true lawmakers, in just the sense George Norris was a lawmaker, but with a good many more strings to their joint bow than Norris had. In addition, these two were the acknowledged leaders of most of the scores of other young men in government of their general type; so all of them constituted an informal but rather closely knit network which gave useful inner cohesion to an outwardly incoherent administration.

Corcoran and Cohen had come to Washington early, and had had a good deal to do with drafting the first Roosevelt Securities Act. In 1934 they had also drafted the much more important Securities Exchange Act setting up the Securities and Exchange Commission as it exists today; and this got them into the White House for the first time. Yet it was not until 1935 that Corcoran, the front man, achieved regular entrée to the White House. He and Ben Cohen then moved up rapidly to become the President's most important advisers on domestic matters, going to Hyde Park so often that Corcoran's incessant long-distance calls soon drove the President's mother to install that pay telephone in her front hall. To round out the picture, it should also be noted that neither Corcoran, nor Cohen, nor the young men in government who were closest to them were economic nationalists or afflicted with planning ambitions or believers in autarchy. As lawmakers, they did not wish to remake the American system. Instead, they wanted the more rational balance between government and business I have already spoken of, and they aimed to get it by setting limits dictated by their conception of the general welfare, and requiring all, including big business, to stay strictly within those limits.

The Second New Deal, the richest period of Corcoran's and Cohen's work at Roosevelt's elbow, produced four great and novel measures, all of which changed the American polity in ways that were then considered earthshaking, although they are completely taken for granted now. The first in the series was the Wagner Labor Relations Act, setting up the National Labor Relations Board. This charter for organized labor was the handiwork of Senator Wagner rather than President Roosevelt and his advisers, for the first Robert F. Wagner was another true lawmaker of George Norris's sort. Initially, Roosevelt had little or no liking for the Wagner Act. Only when he made his basic strategic choice that produced the Second New Deal did he give Wagner's proposed labor law his strong endorsement. It had hung fire until then, as was natural for a bill so loathed by all businessmen which also lacked White House support. But when Roosevelt endorsed it, Wagner's bill soon became law.

Next after the Wagner Act came the Roosevelt measure that is now the most prominent individual feature he contributed to the modern political landscape, the law setting up the existing Social Security system. What he requested was a straight insurance system, in fact what the Social Security system is today, with both employees and employers paying the insurance bills. The resulting taxes on employees were condemned by many young liberals in Washington on the ground that they were regressive and deflationary. The taxes on the employers were also bitterly resented by the business community, and caused another major business-Roosevelt fissure. Roosevelt explained to the young liberals that this was the way it had to be done, if the Social Security system was to be immune to destructive political attack and therefore to be sure to last. And the system was immune, and has lasted until the present, just as Roosevelt predicted. Furthermore, no one supposes that the present actuarial problems will cause the system to be dumped.

Next came the bill that caused the biggest of all the business-Roosevelt fissures, the Holding Company Act, which was the handiwork of Tom Corcoran and Ben Cohen in partnership with the doughty Sam Rayburn of Texas, then House Democratic leader. Just why the whole business class of America so passionately rallied to the defense of the public utilities holding companies, I have never been able to understand. Industrial business, after all, has just as great an interest in low utilities rates as the humblest suburban housewife. But rally the businessmen did, and it was a touch-and-go fight, with one bad defeat for Roosevelt when the most extreme language of the so-called "death sentence" clause was rejected by Congress. None the less, the substance of the bill became law, and thus doom was pronounced against all the larger, less functional holding companies which had been set up for no purpose except, first, to make money on the initial sale of stock at inflated prices, and then by rigging the accounts of their subordinate corporations to justify the inflated prices.

Finally, the last of the four great measures of the Second New Deal was the Banking Act, setting new rules for the Federal Reserve System that are still in force. This led to a long struggle with just one Senator, the aging Carter Glass of Virginia, the father of the original Federal Reserve system. Every time I think of Glass, I find myself wondering why modern politicians of the standing of Carter Glass are almost uniformly bland, homogenized, and uninteresting, like so many samples of commercial cake mix. Glass was unbeatable in his own state as long as he lived, but no one had ever homogenized *him*. He died a stern, unreconstructed Jeffersonian Democrat with a rightwards slant. No matter who opposed him, he told them to go to the devil, and the way he told them was usually acid enough to skin a mule.

Glass was greatly respected in the Senate, and he got much of what he wanted in that struggle in 1935. Yet Roosevelt and Marriner Eccles, the Keynesian banker he had named chairman of the Federal Reserve, got what they chiefly wanted too. The control over the Federal Reserve system by the Federal Reserve Bank of New York and the other main regional banks was broken after nearly a quarter century. The Federal Reserve Board thus became an independent body, with full power over what is now the open market committee and most other aspects of national credit and money policy as well.

The Second New Deal also saw the passage of a series of other measures that seemed important at the time, but they may be passed over, as may the measures resulting from the appearance of the Dust Bowl in the Plains States, which I have already briefly touched upon. If time had permitted, there might have been further measures, for the war between Roosevelt and the businessmen was now being waged in deadly earnest. But 1936, it must be remembered, was an election year, and everything else in the United States always gives way when a national election is coming soon.

The Republican Old Guard was already fighting a rearguard action, and the best indicator of the rearguard action was the party's choice for the Presidential nomination, Alf M. Landon of Kansas. Landon was an excellent Governor of his state, a most pleasant and fine man, and a liberal man, too, by the Republican standards of that era. He is still very much alive as these words are written, and his daughter is a Senator from Kansas. In 1936, however, he had hardly been nominated when his voice, which was not in any case the kind of voice best made for clarion calls, was drowned out by other, more conventional Republican voices. One of these, and not the least loud, was the voice of the victim of Roosevelt's and Alice Longworth's amateur counterespionage, Mrs. Preston Davie. Mrs. Davie had counted the days from Landon's nomination until the election, and the Republican convention was hardly over before she began chanting, day after day in newspapers and sometimes on the radio, "One hundred and sixty-two days to save the American way of life!"—and then the next day "One hundred and sixty-one days," and so on until the votes were counted.

Oddly enough, a great many of the richer Republicans, deluded by the all but unanimously anti-Roosevelt newspapers and by the grossly erroneous *Literary Digest* poll, really believed that Landon would win. I can testify to the delusion because I escaped from mounting difficulties by going to a very grand ball that autumn (at which more than one lady wore a special Mainbocher ball dress embroidered with golden Kansas sunflowers), and I paid off all my accumulated debts by betting $100-even on Roosevelt with all comers. Because they had so deluded themselves, too, it was all the more appalling to the conservative element in the country when Roosevelt carried every state but Maine and Vermont.

The horror of the election result for the conservative element was also greatly increased by two other most significant factors. This was the first election in which organized labor contributed heavily to the funds of the Democrats. John L. Lewis, who was already spearheading a great drive for industrial unionism under the CIO, contributed no less than $469,000 from his United Mineworkers' own funds, while the total contribution of all the CIO unions reached the really gigantic figure of $770,000. It seemed to all right-thinking conservatives that organized labor had bought the Presidency for cash on the barrelhead. Of course it was not true. Later, when Roosevelt refused to take sides in a tense big labor-big business struggle, John L. Lewis, a most pic-

90

turesque fellow with a knack for Biblical prose, thundered at the President: "It ill behooves one who has supped at labor's table to curse with equal fervor and fine impartiality both labor and its adversaries when they are locked in a deadly embrace." Later still, Lewis angrily supported the Republican nominee in 1940. But when conservative Americans begin to panic, their fears often leave very little room for the undramatic practicalities which commonly add up to the truth.

As to the other factor that panicked the conservative element, it was the nature and the trend of Roosevelt's campaign. The keynote was his acceptance speech, in which he denounced "the economic royalists." In his last speech, at Madison Square Garden, he declared roundly, "I should like to have it said of my first administration that in it the forces of selfishness and lust for power have met their match. And I should like to have it said of my second administration that in it these forces have met their master." The applauding roars were deafening.

After the votes were counted, there appeared to be no reason why Roosevelt could not do anything he happened to wish to do as President; for this was the first election in which the old American political pattern disappeared for good. The blacks now voted Democratic for the first time. The "ethnics"—meaning mainly Catholics of all possible non-WASP racial origins—went for Roosevelt to just about the last man and woman. The farmers backed him; the South was passionately loyal to him; and the city bosses turned out their fullest votes for him. Thus the New Deal coalition surfaced for the first time, and when it first surfaced it appeared to be unbeatable. No wonder the flesh of the whole owning class crept horribly all over again when Arthur Krock of the *New York Times* somewhat inaccurately published an alleged warning by Harry Hopkins to one of his rich friends: "We're going to spend and spend, and tax and tax, and elect and elect!" Curiously enough, however, the twilight of the New Deal was already near at hand.

Before describing the New Deal's twilight, however, I propose to take a little while to describe the human scene of Roosevelt's endeavors as President, which was also, so to say, the stage on which the country watched him in action. One must begin with the fact that Washington in the 1930s was still small and safe, and the government in Washington was still on a small and human scale. The best symbol of the change that has overtaken Washington is the ornamental cast iron barrier protecting the White House lawns and grounds. It is now around nine feet high and reinforced in various ways, too. Yet there had been no such barrier until Theodore Roosevelt's time, and he had ordered its installation only to prevent his lawns being used as a public right of way—and had been denounced as unneighborly for his pains. Until the Second World War seemed imminent and the Secret Service insisted upon something higher and more secure, the Theodore Roosevelt barrier remained in place; and it was low enough to be easily vaulted over by a reasonably athletic ten-year-old. I should add that the Second World War barrier was then raised again to its present height because of the Puerto Rican terrorists' attempt to assassinate President Truman while he was living at Blair House during some radical structural reinforcement of the White House.

Although Roosevelt had suffered one assassination attempt at the outset, when Mayor Anton Cermak of Chicago was killed by his side in Miami, the Secret Service in the Roosevelt years was always unobtrusive. Nor did you need security clearance or a special card to enter any building in Washington, including the White House itself. The gates were always open; if you were a newspaperman, you were known to everyone; and you just walked into the Presidential office wing of the White House, hung up your hat in the pressroom, and asked friends, "What's new?"

The same difference of scale and ease of access between the present and the past are apparent in Roosevelt's White House staff and in his famous press conferences—the only ones that ever came close to giving real substance to the cliché about American press conferences having the role of question time in the British Parliament. There literally was no White House staff of the modern type, with policy-making functions. Two extremely pleasant, unassuming, and efficient men, Steve Early and Marvin McIntyre, handled the President's day-to-day schedule and routine, the donkey-work of his press relations, and such like. There was a secretarial camarilla of highly competent and dedicated ladies who were led by "Missy" LeHand, an efficient, very pretty woman who was widely supposed (I never knew whether correctly) to have been the President's resident mistress for a good many years. There were also lesser figures to handle travel arrangements, the enormous flow of correspondence, and the like. But that was that; and national policy was strictly a problem for the President, his advisers of the moment (who had constant access to the President's office but no offices of their own in the White House), and his chosen chiefs of departments and agencies.

As for the famous press conferences, anything of the sort would be totally ruled out now by the enormous inflation of the news-handling business, both in size and self-importance. Today, Presidential press conferences are like vast but occasional circuses, with preening personalities desiring to see themselves on the television screen, all simultaneously screaming for attention, while the unfortunate President of the day struggles to transmit his chosen message to the nation. Roosevelt's press conferences were downright cozy, in contrast, with no one there but seasoned professional reporters, all of whom knew one another and did not wish to make asses of themselves before their colleagues or the President they much liked and admired. There were seldom more of them, furthermore, than a hundred or so, and never, never more than two hundred. Before this intimate congregation, almost all known individually to the President, Roosevelt would sit behind his desk, perpetual cigarette in its holder tilted to the accustomed angle, full of confidence and jokes, and above all giving the reporters much information of value to them and to the country.

The reader may suspect me of nostalgia, and the suspicion is well-founded. Since I have gone so far, I may as well go further. I had the good luck to be assigned to Hyde Park for the weekend of the 1936 election and election night. Those were glorious days, for the countryside—then wholly untouched by developers—was in its highest autumn beauty, rich with all the colors of a cock pheasant in full plumage. The great occasion, however, was election night at the big house—which was in truth not at all big, except for the handsome large living room the President and his mother had added. With great difficulty, Mrs. James Roosevelt had been induced to invite everyone to the election night party: all the reporters like myself, the two or three radio reporters (for there was no television then, of course), the entire White House staff from secretaries to advisers in attendance, all the Secret Service men, even the cameramen—a final group whose inclusion was known to have caused the President's mother to come as close to kicking like a steer as a true lady could ever do. Perhaps because her mother-in-law had so strongly resisted the whole project, the commissary had been left to Eleanor Roosevelt, and therefore largely consisted of damp, dank, ostentatiously dreary roast beef sandwiches. But the President made sure there was plenty to drink, and it was a jolly party.

The President was secluded in the dining room with Steve Early and Marvin McIntyre, following and analyzing the returns coming in on three specially installed press tickers—for even radio, in those days, did not reliably cover the whole country. Mrs. James Roosevelt went among her guests, dispensing graciousness with just a trace of the tone of the lady of the manor reluctantly opening a bazaar she considered unworthy of her presence. Eleanor Roosevelt went about, too, very much herself, at once wonderful and a bit puritanical (she had a way of glancing at the quantities of Scotch in people's glasses) but above all dispensing a warm welcome to all. Ben Cohen wandered here and there dispensing pessimism in his peculiar drawl. ("I'm verrry worrried about Iowaaa.") Tom Corcoran, always ebullient, sang Irish songs and accompanied himself on the accordion. And then the dining doors were opened, for Landon conceded the election very early; and the whole troop formed in line and passed in review before the President seated at the dining room table, cocking his cigarette in its holder as usual, and accepting our congratulations with obvious pleasure.

I think of the evening often, primarily because I do not suppose any American President on any future election night will ever again be able to have another family party—for that was what it was like—of the sort I remember so well. Because of the inflation of the White House staff, plus the inflation of the news-handling business and the rise of television, plus the advent of terrorism and the new requirements of security, a very large hall would have to be hired to hold all those who travel with the President nowadays. Yet there were not more than fifty-plus of us, all told, on that evening in 1936; and we were the entire entourage of the President who had done more in his first term to change the United States than any succeeding President has ever begun to do, or even thought of doing, in his whole period in office. So the question arises whether the American government would not work better, get more done, and in general *be* better if it could be magically reduced to its former human scale again. But of course the question is no longer worth asking.

As for the way the Roosevelts lived in the White House, the description involves a phrase seldom used now; yet the best way to put it is to say that they lived like a rather old-fashioned American gentleman's family in comfortable circumstances. Despite the liveried doormen, in other words, there was nothing in the way they lived that could be said in the smallest degree to be glossy, or particularly conspicuous, or likely to meet with the approval of the new group known as the "beautiful people."

As a young man, the President had always got his suits from an English tailor, as was usual in those days for men of his sort, and I suspect he went on doing so—but he rarely took trouble about what he wore, and he only allowed himself two pairs of new shoes per annum. No one in his senses could have hankered to know, either, which leading New York dressmaker was patronized by Eleanor Roosevelt. Her wedding dress was no doubt ordered from Worth in Paris, for that was then the custom of clans like hers in New York, and her family must have provided her with a trousseau which would pass inspection. But when the trousseau was worn out, one may be certain she never again saw the inside of a leading dressmaker's establishment. As for her hats, on the rare occasions when convention required her to cover her head, they usually had the look of having been recently found under the bed.

Then, too, the White House interiors were no more decorated than Eleanor Roosevelt herself. Shabby things and new things, hideous things and fine things, jostled one another everywhere in the private rooms on the second, or private, floor of the White House, while the walls were all but papered with naval prints from the President's collection. The "beautiful people" would not have felt at home; yet their strongest disdain would surely have been aroused by what appeared on the White House table—in this case with justice.

The drink, being the President's department, was not actively repellent. For a small party, he would usually make the cocktails himself with great gusto, and Harry Hopkins, no innocent in these matters, admitted he made a good old-fashioned and a fair martini—although I remember the martinis as about the color of spar varnish. What wine there was could sometimes be pretty good, but there was not much wine. As for the food, it was notorious.

Eleanor Roosevelt had imported a nutritionist to be the

Presidential housekeeper, and year after year this woman showed once again that nutritionists may well know how to make food healthful, but scorn to make it appetizing or even edible. The salads were especially deplorable; for they tended to be complicated and decorative, and might even conceal bits of marshmallow in their dreadful depths. But all else was pretty depressing too, and Martha Gellhorn once astonished her husband-to-be, Ernest Hemingway, by eating a hearty meal of sandwiches before they went to dinner at the White House together. Nor was she the only precautionary sandwich-eater among those accustomed to the White House cuisine. What the nutritionist perpetrated was only part of the story, moreover. Scrambled eggs are not an easy dish to cook in such a way that hungry men turn away in discouragement, yet the scrambled eggs Eleanor Roosevelt always made in a chafing dish for Sunday night supper were undeniably discouraging.

The oddest aspect of the White House cuisine, none the less, was the fate of the near carloads of pheasant, quail, partridge, reed bird, wild duck, wild turkey, venison, antelope, even terrapin from Maryland, which came into the White House every year from rural areas all over the country. Great numbers of American farmers and ranchers in fact felt enduring gratitude to the President as the man who had personally saved their lands and livelihoods; and this gratitude was annually expressed in presents of game. Since all these birds and beasts were moving proofs of the near-love the President inspired in many Americans, and also very good to eat, you might have supposed the game would have been eaten. Instead, the game always went into the big cellar ice boxes and was never seen on the White House table unless Eleanor Roosevelt happened to be taking one of her innumerable trips, when her husband sometimes asked for a game dinner.

I suspected then and I still suspect that this extreme puritanism about food in a house whose master liked to eat well, and who particularly loved old-fashioned grand food like game, was only partly another manifestation of Eleanor Roosevelt's detestation of anything savoring of worldly ways. She was never against quiet revenges with a moral excuse. She equated plain living with high thinking, so it was moral to eat badly. And if her husband did not like eating badly, why there were passages in their joint past she had not liked either.

48

Inaugural Address —

I am certain that my fellow Americans expect that

on my induction into the Presidency I will address them

with a candor and a decision which the present situation

of our nation impels. This is preeminently the time

to speak the truth, the whole truth, frankly and boldly.

Nor need we shrink from being honest *by facing* as to the condition

of our country today. This great nation will endure

as it has endured, will revive and will prosper. So

first of all let me assert my firm belief that the only

thing we have to fear is fear itself, - nameless, unreasoning,

unjustified terror which paralyzes the needed efforts *needed* to

~~convert retreat into advance.~~

~~In the crisis of our war for Independence; in the~~

~~rivalry, the unrest and the doubts of the early days~~

~~of our constitutional government; later in the dark days~~

~~of the war between the states,~~ a leadership of frankness

and vigor met with that understanding and support of

the people themselves which is essential to victory.

I am convinced that you will again give that support to

Inauguration Day

The 32nd President of the United States took office on 4 March 1933 under appalling circumstances. Most of the country's banks were closed, and the nation was as near to collapse as it had ever been. Glumly, the outgoing President lamented, ''We are at the end of our string.'' It did not seem so to FDR. And it was his confident voice enunciating the now-celebrated words of the First Inaugural Address (above) that filled Americans with a renewed sense of hope. Over millions of radios throughout the country the message came forth clear and strong: ''the only thing we have to fear is fear itself.''

The new team

Roosevelt's Cabinet met for the first time on 5 March 1933.
Seated clockwise around the table from the President are
William H. Woodin (Treasury), Homer S. Cummings (Attorney General), Claude Swanson (Navy), Henry A. Wallace (Agriculture), Frances Perkins (Labor), Daniel C.

Roper (Commerce), Harold L. Ickes (Interior), James A. Farley (Postmaster General), George H. Dern (War), and Cordell Hull (State). Of these, Wallace, Ickes, and Hull, along with Frances Perkins, played particularly important roles in shaping administration policies.

Beginnings

Within a few days of taking office, FDR introduced two regular features of his administration: "fireside chats" by radio to the American people and open press conferences. On March 8, FDR gave his first press conference (above). "I am told," he said to the reporters gathered around his desk, "that what I am about to do will become impossible, but I am going to try it. We are not going to have any more written questions." Over the next twelve years and for 998 press conferences, the President and the White House reporters enjoyed a protracted honeymoon. However much or little FDR divulged, his press conferences were invariably entertaining.

The Hundred Days

During his first three months in office, FDR asked Congress to pass an unprecedented amount of new legislation. This period is known as the Hundred Days. On the very day that Congress met, 9 March 1933, both houses passed and the President signed (opposite, top) the Emergency Banking Relief Act.

51

Another early measure was a bill establishing the Civilian
Conservation Corps. It created employment for young men by
putting them to work planting trees and reclaiming land
blighted by forest fires. On 12 August 1933, FDR visited a
CCC camp in Virginia's Shenandoah Valley. With him (left to
right) are Louis Howe, Harold L. Ickes, and Robert Fechner,
Director of Emergency Conservation Work.

52

53

NRA

In the summer of 1933, the NRA "blue eagle" began appearing all over America. FDR considered the act setting up the National Recovery Administration the most important legislation of the early New Deal. The NRA was meant to stop wasteful competition, encourage better regulated pricing and selling policies, and provide for higher wages and shorter hours throughout the American business community.

The farm crisis

What the NRA was to the business community, the AAA was to the farm community. The Agricultural Adjustment Act, which subsidized farmers for limiting the size of their crops. It helped to make the farming community more solvent while at the same time reducing the enormous surpluses that had depressed produce prices. But

55

ere was no immediate help for the drought and dust
orms which ravaged the Great Plains from the Dako-
s down to Texas in 1934 and again in 1936.

PA and Social Security

obably the most visible of all the New Deal agencies was
e Works Progress Administration. The WPA repaired
ads (below) and built post offices, schools, and airports
the way from Maine to California. The agency also
nded the arts and sponsored adult education programs.
ver the years, it came in for a lot of criticism.
ere was even a new word coined—"boondoggling"—to
scribe the WPA's sometimes eccentric projects. But dur-
g the decade in which it functioned, the WPA kept mil-

56

lions of people off the relief rolls and helped materially to change the face of America.

One New Deal innovation is still very much with us: social security. On signing the Social Security Act on 14 August 1935 (below), Roosevelt noted: "Today a hope of many years' standing is fulfilled. . . . We can never insure one hundred percent of the population against one hundred per cent of the hazards and vicissitudes of life, but we have tried to frame a law which will give some measure of protection to the average citizen and to his family against the loss of a job and against poverty-ridden old age." Soon adult Americans began receiving what has since become a commonplace—their social security numbers.

57

The First Lady

There had never been a First Lady like Eleanor Roosevelt. Ever since FDR's return to politics after the polio attack, she had been his mobile surrogate making on-the-spot investigations and coming back with shrewd assessments. Upon his elevation to the Presidency, Mrs. Roosevelt became an increasingly visible public figure.

Soon she was flying off all over America, gathering material for her newspaper column, "My Day." She went everywhere, including coal mines, as a celebrated *New Yorker* cartoon of the period by Robert Day testifies. She spoke at Chicago's "Century of Progress" exposition in 1933.

59

60

61

62

Alliance with labor

The New Deal galvanized labor into a new mood of militancy. As the economy picked up, workers flocked into unions by the thousands. Soon a rash of strikes were breaking out all over America. The troubles were exacerbated in November 1935 when John L. Lewis resigned from the American Federation of Labor to set up the Committee for Industrial Organization. The difference between them was that the AFL was organized craft by craft while the CIO was organized industry by industry. By strongly, if belatedly, supporting passage of Senator Robert M. Wagner's Labor Relations Act, which played a vital role in building the power of unions, FDR forged an even closer alliance with organized labor. Later Lewis was to fall out with FDR, but the honeymoon was still very much on when Lewis appeared on the platform with the President at Wilkes-Barre, Pennsylvania, in October 1936.

Happy Days Are Here Again

The Democrats' theme song in the New Deal era, played incessantly at their national conventions, was *Happy Days Are Here Again*. It wasn't just a song. There was indeed a new sense of buoyancy in the land.

One turning point came with the end of Prohibition, celebrated in a New York bar (below) on 5 December 1933, the date on which the 18th Amendment was finally repealed. People began to act "crazy" again. There were epidemics of jigsaw puzzles, miniature golf, marathon dancing, and jitterbugging throughout the country.

63

64

Nobody better expressed the new mood of America than FDR, shown swinging himself down some steps outside the White House in 1933. "Once again," he could confidently assert, "the very air of America is exhilarating."

The 1936 campaign

As FDR approached another Presidential campaign, the omens looked excellent for his reelection. But this time he would not have the help of his longtime mentor Louis Howe, who died on 8 April 1936.

Needless to say, Roosevelt was nominated by acclamation at the Democratic National Convention in Philadelphia.

The President campaigned brilliantly and in speech after speech hammered home the theme that "we have only just begun to fight."

His Republican opponent was Governor Alfred ("Alf") M. Landon of Kansas. The very image of middle America, Landon was no match for the architect of the New Deal.

By the time FDR wound up his campaign aboard his special train in Stamford, Connecticut (above), he had the confident look of a winner.

One-third of a nation

FDR's second inaugural took place under pouring rain. But nothing dampened the impact of the challenging address that followed:

"In this nation I see tens of millions of its citizens—a substantial part of its whole population—who at this very moment are denied the greater part of what the very lowest standards of today call the necessities of life.

"I see millions of families trying to live on incomes so meager that the pall of family disaster hangs over them day by day.

"I see millions whose daily lives in city and on farm continue under conditions labeled indecent by a so-called polite society half a century ago.

"I see millions denied education, recreation, and the opportunity to better their lot and the lot of their children.

"I see millions lacking the means to buy the products of farm and factory and by their poverty denying work and productiveness to many other millions.

"I see one-third of a nation ill-housed, ill-clad, ill-nourished

"It is not in despair that I paint you that picture. I paint it for you in hope—because the Nation, seeing and understanding the injustice in it, proposes to paint it out. . . ."

espite FDR's confidence, many Americans believed that
ew Deal legislation was improperly fettering the country.
lore ominously, the Supreme Court had declared such key
rograms as the NRA and the AAA unconstitutional. Embold-
1ed by his sweeping victory in the 1936 election, Roosevelt
oposed to "pack" the Court with six additional justices. It
as FDR's first serious miscalculation. His plan to reorganize
1e Supreme Court encountered intense opposition, and by
idsummer it had been effectively shelved. Roosevelt later
aimed to have won the battle; the Court started voting his
ay and several of the more conservative justices soon de-
ded to resign.

long with the hue and cry over the Supreme Court came
1 outbreak of worrisome labor troubles. There were sit-
)wn strikes in auto factories, mass demonstrations, unofficial
)ppages, and violent clashes between workers and police.
1e New Deal had sailed into a sea of troubles.

Adolf Hitler came to power in Germany just five weeks before the start of Roosevelt's first term. In the early days of the New Deal, FDR had gone along with the prevailingly isolationist mood of the country. But by 1937 the time had come to sound a warning. On October 5 Roosevelt launched a trial balloon: "The peace, the freedom, and the security of ninety per cent of the population of the world is being jeopardized by the remaining ten per cent who are threatening a breakdown of all international order and law. . . . When an epidemic of physical disease starts to spread, the community approves and joins in a quarantine of the patients in order to protect the health of the community. . . ." Would it not make sense, the President seemed to be suggesting, for the peace-loving community to quarantine the aggressors?

All in all, it was a fairly vague statement. Nevertheless, the speech stirred up a tumult of opposition. The *Wall Street Journal* advised the President to "stop foreign meddling," and a few isolationist Congressmen even threatened impeachment. FDR prudently beat a retreat.

The epidemic of international lawlessness did not abate. As the summer of 1939 wore on, war seemed increasingly inevitable, although the President was telling reporters in a press conference (opposite) as late as August 25 that hostilities could still be avoided. Then on September 1, the Nazis marched into Poland. Two days later, Britain and France responded by declaring war on Germany.

A step away from isolationism came in September 1940 with the passage of the Selective Service Act, which called for the compulsory military training of American men reaching the age of 21. The President looked on as a blind-folded Henry L. Stimson, Secretary of War, drew the first draft numbers on 29 October 1940.

A third term?

Ever since his reelection in 1936, FDR had kept the party, the press, and the people guessing. Would he—could he—break with long-standing tradition and seek a third term as President?

Events abroad helped to clarify the issue. In ten devastating weeks, beginning 9 April 1940, Hitler's forces overran Denmark, Norway, Holland, Belgium, and France, leaving Britain to sustain the struggle against the Nazi domination of Europe single-handed. It was no time to falter, and Roosevelt did nothing to discourage those who were working to engineer a third-term draft.

I WANT YOU
F.D.R.

STAY AND FINISH THE JOB!

70

When the Democratic National Convention opened at the Chicago Stadium on 15 July 1940, FDR was virtually drafted by acclamation.

Campaigning against Willkie

The Republicans had nominated a most attractive candidate: Wendell Willkie, a successful self-made businessman, ten years younger than FDR, who had become an impressively articulate critic of New Deal economic policies. He was by far the most dangerous opponent Roosevelt had faced. A native of Elwood, Indiana, Willkie is pictured greeting the folks in his home town at the start of his campaign (opposite, top).

71

NO MAN IS GOOD THREE TIMES

72

However, when the election returns were counted, the President had decisively won his third term—27,243,466 votes to Willkie's 22,304,755.

Appointment in Argentia

On 9 August 1941 two naval vessels rode at anchor in the harbor of Argentia off the coast of Newfoundland. One was the British battleship *Prince of Wales* carrying Prime Minister Winston Churchill; the other was the American cruiser *Augusta* carrying President Roosevelt. For three days the two leaders and their staffs held a series of meetings.

Out of the meetings there emerged a joint statement on war aims known as the Atlantic Charter. The eight-point declara-

tion set forth "certain common principles in the national policies of their respective countries on which they base their hopes for a better future for the world."

Sparring for time

Throughout the late summer and autumn of 1941, FDR and Secretary of State Cordell Hull carried on diplomatic negotiations with Japan. With Hitler in control of the European Continent, battering at the gates of Moscow, and menacing the convoys to Britain, the United States needed peace and stability in the Pacific. On 17 November 1941, Ambassador Nomura, Hull, and special envoy Saburu Kurusu (holding cane, below)

t with FDR in the White House. Nothing was accomplished
: the talks continued.

)n 22 November 1941, an intercepted message to Nomura
1 Kurusu warned the diplomats that in a week "things are
omatically going to happen." To Churchill, FDR cabled:
'e must all be prepared for real trouble, possibly soon." But
U.S. Navy, berthed at Pearl Harbor, was not prepared.
rly on Sunday morning, 7 December 1941, Japanese dive
nbers and torpedo bombers attacked the fleet and airfields
re, inflicting grievous damage.

y of infamy

the morrow of the Pearl Harbor attack, Roosevelt ap-
ared before Congress to call for a declaration of war. He
rked on the short speech until the last minute, adding new
ases and substituting words as he went along. A draft with
President's penciled emendations shows that the most me-
rable phrase in the speech—"a date which will live in
amy"—was an afterthought.

uddenly, all the acrimony and disunity of the past year
re forgotten. Thirty-three minutes after Roosevelt had fin-
ed speaking, the Congress passed a resolution declaring
t a state of war existed between the United States and Ja-
.

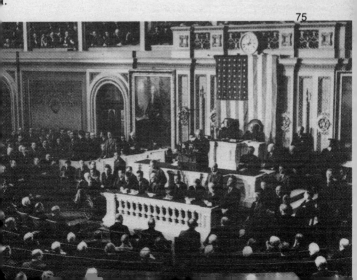

War leader

For months the news was all bad. At Pearl Harbor the Pacific fleet had been severely crippled. Wake Island and Guam fell quickly to the Japanese. Then came the agonizing defeat of U.S. forces in the Philippines. For the first time within living memory, Americans were being badly defeated by a foreign enemy.

To help restore the nation's confidence, FDR announced a fireside chat on the conduct of the war for 23 February 1942. He asked in advance that his listeners have a map of the world ready for reference. To his speech writer Samuel I. Rosenman he said: "I want to explain the war in laymen's language; if they understand the problem and what we are driving at, I am sure that they can take any kind of bad news right on the chin." FDR posed for a photo (above) just before delivering this fireside chat, which Rosenman felt was the most effective one he had ever given.

11 January 1943 the President boarded a Pan American
:pper bound for Casablanca in North Africa. It was a
·cedent-breaking journey. Never before had a President left
: United States in wartime, and not since Lincoln had a
:sident entered a war zone.

⁻or ten days in Casablanca, FDR and Churchill—together
h their chiefs of staff—thrashed out the strategic priorities
:he European theater of operations. When it was all over,
correspondents gathered for an *al fresco* press conference.

79

Fala

Margaret Suckley, a remote cousin, was often with the President during the war years, and it is to her that we owe this informal snapshot of Fala, FDR's famous Scottie.

Fala was a gift to the President from Miss Suckley (still living in retirement near Hyde Park). Fala and FDR were inseparable, and in the 1944 campaign the dog provided the inspiration for one of Roosevelt's wittiest sallies. In a speech lashing out at the opposition's maladroit charges, FDR's voice suddenly took on a tone of mock solemnity: "These Republican leaders have not been content with attacks—on me, or my wife, or on my sons. No, not content with that, they now include my little dog, Fala. Well, of course, I don't resent attacks, and my family doesn't resent attacks, but Fala *does* resent them. You know—you know—Fala's Scotch, and being a Scottie, as soon as he learned that the Republican fiction writers in Congress and out had concocted a story that I had left him behind on an Aleutian Island and had sent a destroyer back to find him—at a cost to the taxpayers of two or three, eight or twenty million dollars—his Scotch soul was furious. He has not been the same dog since."

Mediterranean mission

The year 1943, which began with FDR's trip to Casablanca, ended with his far longer journey to Teheran, with stops in between at Oran, Tunis, Cairo, and—on the way back—Sicily. Teheran was the venue for the first of the Big Three conferences between Stalin, Roosevelt, and Churchill. There plans were coordinated for the vital military moves scheduled for the following spring. In Cairo he met with Generalissimo and Madame Chiang Kai-shek, and in Sicily with General Eisenhower (next page, with FDR's plane in the background).

Shortly after returning from Teheran, the President's health began to give serious cause for alarm. A check-up revealed that he was suffering from a gravely weakened heart and hardening of the arteries. From now on a cardiologist was to be in constant attendance.

81

82

The last campaign

With the war drawing to a climax in 1944, there was never any doubt that Roosevelt would run once again for reelection. But he warned: "I shall not campaign, in the usual sense, for the office. In these days of tragic sorrow, I do not consider it fitting. And besides, in these days of global warfare, I shall not be able to find the time."

In the event he did find time to make campaign speeches in several key cities. Never had FDR impaled his critics more adroitly or brilliantly, and his splendid form as a speaker together with his apparent stamina on the campaign trail served to allay apprehensions about his health.

83

The most grueling day was in New York City on 21 October 1944, when Roosevelt drove for hours through the cold rain in an open limousine as thousands lined the streets from the Bronx down to Lower Manhattan to catch a glimpse of their President. Mrs. Roosevelt noted: "I was really worried . . . but instead of being exhausted he was exhilarated."

On election night there were the usual felicitations at Hyde Park. Once again Roosevelt had defeated his Republican opponent (on this occasion, Governor Thomas E. Dewey of New York) by a wide margin, 432 electoral votes to 99.

Enter Harry Truman

At the Democratic convention in 1944, the choice of FDR's running mate was of paramount importance. Robert E. Hannegan, chairman of the Democratic National Committee, strongly favored the Senator from Missouri, Harry S. Truman, who had made a strong impression as head of a committee investigating war production. FDR ostensibly kept himself aloof from the politicking, and Truman duly got the nomination. A month later, FDR and HST lunched together on the south

lawn of the White House (above). It was one of the very few times the President and his eventual successor were together.

Yalta

Three days after his fourth inaugural, FDR boarded the cruiser *Quincy* for the first leg of his journey to Yalta. The President was visibly fatigued by the time the ship docked in Malta, but he was out on deck with his physician Vice-Admiral Ross McIntyre and his close adviser James F. Byrnes (opposite, top) to survey the island that had sustained so much aerial punishment since the early days of the war. From Malta the President flew on to the Crimea, where for eight days in early February he met with Churchill, Stalin, and such key figures as Anthony Eden and Vyacheslav Molotov. Roosevelt left the Yalta Conference persuaded that broad agreement on the major issues had been reached. But the strain on him was all too apparent in the official photographs that were released after the conference. To a shocked world, they revealed a President looking alarmingly haggard and drawn.

85

86

87

88

Final Report to Congress

On 1 March 1945, two days after his return to Washington, th
President appeared before a joint session of Congress to repc
on the Yalta Conference. A hush fell over the House of Repr
sentatives as FDR was wheeled to a chair and table below th
rostrum.

It was not the same man that the Congress had known
years, or even months, before.

At the end of his speech he mustered his flagging energy to
make a last plea for the United Nations Conference, which
would open eight weeks later in San Francisco: "Peace can
endure only so long as humanity really insists upon it, and is
willing to work for it, and sacrifice for it. Twenty-five years
ago, American fighting men looked to the statesmen of the
world to finish the work of peace for which they fought and
suffered. We failed them. We cannot fail them again and expect the world to survive. . . . "

Then, as the Congress rose to a standing ovation, the Presi
dent slid onto his armless wheelchair and was rolled out.
Many in the audience felt instinctively that they would never
see him there again.

"As soon as I can," Roosevelt told Harry Truman, "I will go
Warm Springs for a rest. I can be in trim again if I stay
ere for two or three weeks." Those close to him prayed that
would be so. In the past FDR had shown remarkable recu-
erative powers, and Warm Springs was the ideal place for
m to rest and relax. He arrived there on 30 March 1945, and
ter a few days in the warm sun his color and spirits were
uch improved. In the mornings he would wheel himself to a
rdtable on the terrace and go over the day's mail with his
cretary Grace Tully (below). But it was a brief respite. On
pril 12, the world learned that FDR had died.

89

The funeral cortege—Hyde Park, 15 April 1945.
Eleanor Roosevelt and her daughter Anna.

All the same, I cannot recall the Roosevelt White House today without a severe spasm of nostalgia. I was not asked there often—usually for the family festivals each year, sometimes for the regular Sunday suppers, more rarely when one of my mother's visits to Washington or something similar provided a special pretext. But on all occasions when I could form a judgment—and leaving the food aside—the style of life in the White House in the Roosevelt years struck me as pretty close to the perfect style of an American President.

For one thing, the interior decorators had not yet laid their fell hands upon the state rooms, in the way that began under President Truman. Hence the rooms were about as Theodore Roosevelt and Stanford White had left them in 1908; and I remember them as rather better than they have ever been since. But above all, both Roosevelts were always warmly welcoming, totally unpretentious, and easy with their guests in precisely the right way. The company was usually haphazardly mixed—old friends, high officials, the odd distinguished foreigner, members of the family, often one or two of the waifs and strays Eleanor Roosevelt had a habit of picking up here and there on her trips—but the company was seldom dull and no one was ever asked for mere show. The state rooms were as grand as the White House state rooms ought to be; but even on major occasions, no attempt was made to heighten the grandeur by stiffness or false fanfare or an atmosphere of fake reverence. The simple, generous hospitality of an old-fashioned American gentleman's house was always the note, even if the food was a flaw. Barring the Roosevelt-haters, most Americans were proud of the Roosevelt White House, and in my opinion they were dead right to be proud.

STORMY WEATHER

From his overwhelming triumph in 1936, Franklin Roosevelt returned to Washington not only elated by success but also overconfident and angry. The anger was directed at the Supreme Court, and entirely understandably. But to make what happened understandable, the composition of the Supreme Court in 1936 must first be understood.

The liberal wing of the Court was composed of three unusually distinguished Justices, Louis D. Brandeis, Benjamin N. Cardozo, and Harlan Fiske Stone. On the right were four reactionaries of an extreme character all but unknown in present-day America, Justices James C. McReynolds, Pierce Butler, Willis J. Van Devanter, and George Sutherland. And in the middle were Owen Roberts and the Chief Justice, Charles Evans Hughes. In the first year or so of the Roosevelt administration, Hughes and Roberts seemed unlikely to join their reactionary brethren, although New Deal measures soon began to stimulate innumerable suits brought by big businessmen with the aim of getting distasteful legislation condemned as unconstitutional. Then in 1935, Justice Roberts, one of the men in the middle, began to join the Court's reactionaries with some regularity, and the Chief Justice sided with the resulting majority of the Court more often than not. Thus by the end of 1936, every New Deal measure still surviving appeared to be in imminent danger; for the majority of the Justices had already come perilously close to holding that any social legislation, of whatever sort, was beyond the permitted limits. This was grave, for the Supreme Court was doing nothing less than nullifying the decisions of an immensely popular President supported by immense Congressional majorities, and the nullifications promised to continue, too. Hence there appeared to be nowhere the President could turn.

It can be seen why Roosevelt was angry. Unfortunately, the President's anger was now equaled by his overconfidence, and overconfidence was supremely risky for anyone wishing to discipline the Supreme Court. For many decades, the sanctity and dignity of the Court had been proclaimed by editorial writers, historians, theorists, and educators; and the sanctity was an accepted fact in the minds of a large majority of Americans. When the President had publicly denounced the NRA decision of 1935 for taking the country back to the time of the "horse and buggy," he had met with the kind of chilly reception that should have warned him. But he was heedless of the warning, or rather, he only took note of it by his extreme secretiveness until he had a bill ready.

The secretiveness led him to consult literally no one about the problem of the Court after the election but his Attorney General, Homer Cummings, an astute Connecticut politician but no towering legal genius. The result was the bill Cummings drafted, which was transparently too clever by half. Its basic provisions were simple enough. They made it possible for members of the federal bench to retire without loss of income, and also authorized the President to add six Justices to the Supreme Court. The real trouble was the President's delighted acceptance of his Attorney General's fairly sleazy proposals for presenting the bill. In the presentation, Roosevelt therefore claimed that the Supreme Court had fallen far behind in its work, which was totally untrue. The Court's alleged delays were further explained on the grounds of the near-senility of some of the Justices, whereas all of them were well known to be notably vigorous—in fact, only too eager to prove their power to serve on the Court long enough to prevent Roosevelt appointing their successors. Nowhere, in sum, did the President confront the real issue, which was the obvious need to transform the Court by one means or another. Instead he piously denied his own obvious aim, which was to transform the Court by packing it with additional Justices of his own choosing.

No one could even pretend to be convinced by this approach, and this gave the President's opponents a huge tactical advantage from the start. At the time, I wrote a history of the Court fight with Turner Catledge of the *New York Times*. I think I knew the drama's ins and outs and narrow balances as well as any man in Washington. Yet even then I could never decide whether the President might have avoided most of his subsequent difficulties by getting a more soundly drafted bill from Ben Cohen and Tom Corcoran, and above all, by adopting a completely forthright and high-principled approach. As it was, the fight over the President's Court bill was the longest, most sustained, and most dramatic struggle which has taken place in Congress in the 20th century, and it was also the only fight in Congress in my memory ever to give rise to a genuine and prolonged debate of deep interest.

What nourished the excitement was the way the opposition to the bill first recovered from the dismay caused by surprise, and then gained strength, week by week, until the President was being actively opposed by all sorts of men whose support he had been able to count on with certainty for the previous four years. It was worth watching too—and the whole country watched each week's events with breathless interest—because the fight centered in the Senate, which always puts on a better show than the House. Finally, the drama was heightened to the utmost because Roosevelt had every reason to expect to win the fight at the outset, and he remained the probable winner until the wholly unforeseen grand climax began.

Modern historians are so given to using misleading political stereotypes that it may be useful to point out that besides the numerically enormous Democratic majorities in the Senate and House, there was another reason Roosevelt seemed almost sure to win. The traditional Democrats of the South are now commonly portrayed as having always been deep-dyed conservatives; but with few exceptions like Carter Glass of Virginia, the Southern Senators and Representatives had been the most dependable, if not the most ideological, Roosevelt supporters on Capitol Hill all through the President's first four years in office.

Southerners, as I have said already, also composed virtually the entire Congressional leadership of those days, and in the Senate all three key men in leadership positions were Southerners. The first and foremost was the majority leader, Joseph T. Robinson of Arkansas, who exercised a more absolute authority over the Senate than even Lyndon B. Johnson later enjoyed. Robinson's partners were the Democratic whip, James F. Byrnes of South Carolina, and the shrewd and entertaining chairman of the Senate Finance Committee, Pat Harrison of Mississippi. From start to finish, Senators

Robinson, Byrnes, and Harrison did all they could to get the President the Court bill he wanted.

In those days, furthermore, the low level of wages and the seemingly endemic unemployment gave federal patronage great political weight it has now lost. By dispensing White House-provided jobs and other patronage plums with extreme acumen, Senator Robinson alone had accumulated enough political IOUs from other Democratic Senators to have passed the Court bill all but single-handed if the IOUs had ever been cashed. Before long, too, the management of the bill was vastly improved when Roosevelt transferred this responsibility from Homer Cummings to the Corcoran-Cohen partnership; and with discreet advice from Robinson, Byrnes, and Harrison, Tom Corcoran passed whole bowls-full of federal plums wherever patronage could do any good in a Senatorial office not as yet covered by Senator Robinson.

With these advantages, Roosevelt was not worried about the vigor of the debate in the Senate, or the vocal opposition to the Court bill in the country, or the all but unanimous outrage of the newspapers. First of all, however, he had underrated, even virtually ignored, the man who turned out to be his most effective antagonist. Chief Justice Hughes, with his fine features, his erect carriage, his patriarchal but well-trimmed beard, looked remarkably like a whole series of Renaissance portrayals of the senior member of the Trinity. In reality, the Jehovah-like exterior concealed a truly formidable political infighter—and Hughes was determined to see Roosevelt's Court bill fail.

At just the right moment, therefore, the Chief Justice submitted a letter proving, coldly and in deadly detail, the complete falsity of Roosevelt's charge that the Court had fallen far behind in its proper work. Although the Hughes letter piously excluded any discussion of issues rather than facts, it did Roosevelt's cause much harm. Worse still, however, was the sudden change in the Court's direction, which Hughes contrived by the simple expedient of refusing to side with the reactionary Justices any longer, and more important, by persuading Justice Roberts to do the same thing. Not only the President, but also Cummings, Cohen, Corcoran, and the other Presidential strategists had counted on the Supreme Court to give the Court bill more and more impetus by throwing out more and more major New Deal measures throughout its spring term, when the big decisions are usually handed down. Just the opposite happened, and the Court bill's loss of impetus was so great that even the Senators most loyal to Roosevelt began to mutter about the need for compromise.

Even so, Roosevelt "had his Dutch up," as he was fond of saying. He would not think of compromise while he could still count on those political IOUs in Senator Robinson's pocket and his own pocket. Robinson's lifelong ambition was to sit on the Supreme Court himself, and Roosevelt had hinted that Robinson could confidently expect one of the new Justices' places after the Court bill had passed. With single-minded purpose, the majority leader had therefore carried on the battle, day after day and week after week, often giving the Court bill twelve hours or more of his work each day, throughout the long months that the bill had been before the Senate.

As late as the end of May 1937, and largely by Robinson's efforts, the President had ample Senate votes in hand to put through a reasonable compromise on the Court bill, reducing the number of new Justices to be appointed from six to two or three. This would have been ample for all practical purposes in view of the Hughes-Roberts switch, as a result of which the Wagner Labor Relations Act had just been held constitutional. But at this juncture, Senator Burton K. Wheeler, a former great White House friend in the Senate and now bitterly anti-Roosevelt, joined with Senator William Borah of Idaho to contrive the resignation of Justice Willis Van Devanter.

The resulting vacancy on the Court automatically put the President in a cleft stick. When the news of the Van Devanter resignation broke, the entire Senate flocked around Joe Robinson's desk, congratulating the majority leader on his coming promotion and calling him "Mr. Justice." But Senator Robinson, although acceptable as one of six new Justices, was far too innately conservative to be acceptable all by himself, either to the President's New Deal advisers and strategists or to liberal groups in the country. Consequently the President very foolishly treated this man—who had served him most usefully and with absolute fidelity for four and a half years—as though he were the most shameful sort of poor relation, too embarrassing to be publicly acknowledged. The Senate was enraged. The whole outlook

102

darkened continuously for two long weeks, and finally the President had to face hard facts.

He therefore approached Robinson through an intermediary, invited him to the White House, made him the offer he had been longing to hear for so long, and authorized him to work out the best compromise he could. Robinson went off to tackle this thorny task with a light heart, but it was now too late, simply because the Court fight had already taken too much out of the Senate leader. He was a big, bull-like, red-faced, plethoric man with an awe-inspiring temper needing constant control. Such men, when they have reached Robinson's age, are always in danger if exhausted, and he had reached the end of his life-tether when he walked home from the Capitol on the night of 13 July to his apartment across the park in the Methodist Building.

As Mrs. Robinson was at home in Arkansas, the Senator went to bed alone with a copy of the *Congressional Record* of the previous day—his usual bedtime reading. A massive heart attack then struck him before he began to feel like sleeping, and he evidently struggled out of bed in the hope of getting help. It was no use. On the morning of 14 July 1937, the terrified maid and apartment-house elevator boy found Robinson lying on the floor by his bed, the *Congressional Record* fallen beside him, and the electric light still burning. That was the real end of the Court fight, for it is the nature of all political IOUs to die when the holder of the IOUs dies or leaves Congress; and thus the President's last hope of passing any real semblance of his Court bill was dead with the great IOU-holder, Joseph T. Robinson.

The desertion of Roosevelt's cause by large numbers of Senators whose votes he had counted on to the last, and the passage of the thinnest sort of face-saving bill making better retirement provisions for Justices and lower court judges, were the routine sequels of the death of Senator Robinson. But there was another sequel, wholly unnoticed at the time, which was far from being routine. As it turned out, the fight over the Roosevelt Court bill became another unwritten amendment to the Constitution of the United States.

With the exception of the Bill of Rights, all the Constitution's more important amendments have been unwritten. No one ever says this, but if you think about it, Andrew Jackson was an amendment in himself, for his Presidency permanently established the political party system which the authors of the Constitution had tried so hard to guard against. The Civil War was another vital amendment; for the defeat of the South permanently determined the true relationship between the states and the federal government. In the same way, the unsuccessful Court bill was still another such amendment, for the fight over it permanently determined the true relationship between the Judicial branch of the government on the one hand and the Executive and Legislative branches on the other.

Before the Court fight, the Supreme Court had increasingly claimed for itself a higher right to decide upon national policy, surpassing the combined rights of the President and the Congress. But since the historic switch of the Chief Justice and Justice Roberts, which did so much to defeat the President's bill, the Supreme Court has never again claimed this higher policy-making power in any serious way. During the Chief Justiceship of Earl Warren, social policies of various sorts were undoubtedly originated by the Court, yet they were never policies the incumbent President and the Congressional majority actively disapproved. At present, moreover, a changed Supreme Court is engaged in considerably amending the social policies almost solely born of their predecessors' decisions.

Thus the rule that the Court's task is to adjudicate but not to legislate—the rule advocated by Justice Holmes and Justice Frankfurter and Franklin Roosevelt too—has become the key to the role of the government's judicial branch, apparently for good. This now gives great pain to the liberal ideologists who wish to see their aims attained the easy way; but these people have never learned another, even more basic, rule, well understood by Roosevelt, Frankfurter, and Holmes. This is the rule that the only *right* way for things to get done in America is with the support of a majority of the electorate.

For these reasons, President Roosevelt used to claim, later on, that he was really the victor of the Court fight. He was right structurally, and he might even have avoided any serious long-term political loss if the outcome had not made him vengeful. As a Senate reporter, I am proud to say, I made a close friend of Hugo Black, and he remained my friend until he died. Yet no sane man can doubt that Roosevelt chose Black for the first Supreme Court vacancy partly as a revenge on the Senate. He was the most left-wing Senator of those days, and his nomination therefore offered other Senators the most unpalatable nominee they would surely have to confirm. Roosevelt's choice of Black left scars, too, but nothing like the scars that were left by his almost open intervention in the Senate's struggle over the succession to the vacant majority leadership.

The strongest claim to Joseph T. Robinson's empty place as majority leader was that of the chairman of the Senate Finance Committee, Pat Harrison. As previously noted, Harrison had supported Roosevelt on the Court bill, and he had also voted for the Roosevelt measures with regularity during the first four years. But he had argued with Roosevelt about tax policy when the President did not feel like arguing and, worse still, he had positively refused to go down the line for a tax bill aimed at making the rich pay a bit more, which Roosevelt wanted and most of the Senators did not want. So Roosevelt set out to block the choice of Harrison by throwing his weight behind the rival candidacy of Senator Alben W. Barkley of Kentucky, whom he regarded as dependable and completely biddable. In my opinion, this was one of the President's most serious failures of short-term political judgment.

There is no doubt at all that Harrison was not a liberal, as the President's young liberal advisers kept declaiming at the White House. But he was a kindly, humorous, extremely quick-minded man with great influence in the Senate, and he was an instinctively loyal Democrat. There was every reason to expect, therefore, that Harrison, if rightly handled, would serve Roosevelt just as well in the role of majority leader as Robinson of Arkansas, a man with identical opinions, had served the President for so long. Barkley was a good man, too, but the President's aid for Barkley, who won, left the Senate with a double dose of bad feelings, because of the personal bitterness engendered by the Court fight and the widespread institutional bitterness caused by Roosevelt's interference in Senate affairs.

There were serious bad feelings in the House, too, and this anti-Roosevelt sentiment on Capitol Hill caused the development that became the long-enduring penalty for the Court fight. This first fruit of the new anti-Roosevelt sentiment was the conservative coalition, which was informally organized almost at once. Thereafter Roosevelt's problem in Congress was no longer happily restricted to outvoting the much-weakened Republicans. The coalition brought the Republicans together with a considerable number of the more conservative Democrats, mainly from the South, and the two groups concerted their votes. The combination was long-lasting, and the penalty for the Court fight was therefore paid by installments, and not just by Roosevelt either. Further installments also had to be paid by two of Roosevelt's Democratic successors in the White House, Presidents Truman and Kennedy; and as these words are written, the liberal Democrats in Congress are paying again because the conservative coalition has been re-formed in the House of Representatives to support President Reagan.

Much of the legislatively useful period of 1937 was occupied by the Court fight, and the resulting bad feelings, plus the conservative coalition, combined to make the 1938 Congressional session relatively sterile except for routine work. Meanwhile Roosevelt and his young advisers were maturing the plan that could well have reduced Roosevelt to near impotence in 1939–40, and then have made an unprecedented third term entirely out of the question for him. This did not happen, but only because the danger abroad soon grew so great and came so close that the President was forced to deal with the danger as best he could; and this in turn forcibly shifted American politics to an entirely new battlefield, with a wholly new alignment of forces in the battle. Yet the plan the President, Tom Corcoran, Ben Cohen, and one or two more of his advisers matured in 1938, mainly in response to the conservative coalition, is still worth examining for the light it throws on the present and the lesson it gives for the future.

The lesson—to put the cart before the horse—was that disaster must always follow when any American leader or group seeks to remold one of our disorderly major political parties on purer, more orderly ideological lines. In the years from 1965 through 1980, the liberal left wing of the Democratic Party made a sustained experiment with ideological remolding, and anyone who supposes this attempt did not lead to disaster for those who made it need only look at the consequences in the Washington of the Reagan administration. It must be added that in 1938, when Roosevelt tried to do much the same thing, the effort was based on much more sane and practical calculations of electoral realities.

In the wake of the 1936 election, after all, it was rather natural to hope that the Democratic Party could be remolded into a New Deal-Roosevelt party. In no part of the country in 1936 had the President won stronger support than in the

106

South, and it even seemed possible that in many Southern states majorities would be found for Roosevelt-style New Deal Democrats instead of the traditional Democrats the Southerners had elected for so long. To be fair to the President, his advisers of that period were, if anything, more misguided. All believed a political realignment on ideological lines was justified by the results of the 1936 vote. The President can have heard few warnings, in fact, except from those whose advice he was inclined to discount, primarily Vice President Garner and the President's own overall political manager of former days, Jim Farley, who was no longer really close to the White House by 1938.

Hence Roosevelt pushed ahead with the so-called "purge" attempt in the Congressional election of 1938. The word "purge" may seem poorly justified, since the President mainly sought to defeat a carefully chosen trio of members of his own party who had joined the conservative coalition. Yet if those men had been successfully attacked, the result would have been to change the whole pattern of American politics. Precisely this happened for a while when the unscrupulous Joseph R. McCarthy went to work in Maryland to defeat Senator Millard Tydings. Senator McCarthy terrorized the Congress for a while after Tydings was beaten, simply because his colleagues feared him in the aftermath of the Tydings defeat. But Roosevelt was no McCarthy. The only casualty of the Roosevelt purge was a vulnerable New York Congressman; while Senator Tydings, under attack this time as later, survived comfortably, and so did the revered senior Democrat from the South, Senator Walter George of Georgia.

As was only natural, the attempted but unsuccessful purge of ideological sinners in 1938 left another large deposit of ill will in Congress and elsewhere. It says much for the strength of conviction and national feeling of the Senators and Representatives Roosevelt had so alienated that very large numbers of them, with the Southerners leading the van, then rallied to the President's support when the great issue became dealing with the threat of Adolf Hitler and his allies.

The time has now come to make the change Roosevelt himself described, in the language previously quoted, as the replacement of "Dr. New Deal" by "Dr. Win the War." But I cannot turn to another subject without trying very briefly to sum up the nature of Roosevelt's achievement in his first six years in the White House; for it seems to me fair to say that

107

no other President except George Washington, the founder, has ever changed the face of this country so greatly.

First, consider the massive list of boldly innovating measures of reform and social betterment which Franklin Roosevelt sponsored. Then tick off the names of the new governmental institutions he founded, so many of which still play a useful role. After that, reflect upon the remarkable fact that this one man first corrected the balance between government and business, so that national policy at length began to be made by the elected national government, and then went on—admittedly a bit ham-handedly—to correct the temporarily disordered balance between the constitutionally established great branches of the national government itself! This is a record of creativity without parallel in American history at any time since the first acts of creation which produced the United States; I also believe there is no parallel to it in any other free society in the 20th century. Finally, in judging Roosevelt one must throw into the balance that wonderful though somewhat inchoate process I have particularly stressed, the inclusion of the excluded. This greatest of all Roosevelt's contributions was made possible only by the successes of Roosevelt's first six years, although it did not reach maturity until the war years.

To judge the extraordinary dimensions of Roosevelt's achievement from 1939 to 1941, and in the war years until his death in 1945, one must first take note of the mountainous difficulties he had to surmount. One difficulty was practical. The Congressional elections of 1938 brought Roosevelt his first severe setback at the polls since the election of 1932. From his victory in his campaign against Herbert Hoover, he had always gone forward with an army growing greater in numbers behind him. But 1938 was a Republican year, for there were extremely substantial Republican gains in both House and Senate. These gains, plus Roosevelt's own defeat in his attempted Democratic purge, inevitably and most significantly strengthened the new conservative coalition. In addition, new Republican leaders who would be important in the future, like Senator Robert A. Taft of Ohio and Senator Henry Cabot Lodge of Massachusetts, now made their first appearances at the Capitol. All outward signs indicated, in sum, that the political balance had tilted rather radically against the President.

Yet what may be called the President's atmospheric difficulty very greatly outweighed the practical political difficulty resulting from declining power on Capitol Hill and within his party. The prevailing intellectual atmosphere of the United States was in fact heavily and apparently unshakably hostile to the kinds of measures required by the ever-growing threat in the rest of the world. It would be needlessly space-consuming to try to document in detail the follies that gave rise to this hostile atmosphere which Roosevelt was called upon to transform, and thus to rescue his country a second time. It will be enough to describe and analyze my own beginning experience in Washington.

My first serious assignment as a Senate reporter was to cover the second "Nye hearings," as they were called. They got their name from their prime mover, Senator Gerald P. Nye, a Republican pseudo-progressive from North Dakota. Nye was an unappetizing man who later became Adolf Hitler's strongest defender in the Senate, and further revealed a strong streak of exceedingly nasty anti-Semitism; but previous to this phase he had made himself the hero of many liberal intellectuals. The liberal intellectuals were still near-pacifists in those days, and Nye had staked out "neutrality"—meaning avoidance of war at all costs—as his patented political property.

The first Nye hearings had already taken place before I came to Washington. J. Pierpont Morgan, expected with awe as a dread apparition of financial power, had taken the stand at the first Nye hearings before the 1936 election, and had ended by appearing a kindly but somewhat victimized elderly gentleman. Some initial "neutrality" legislation had also resulted from the first Nye hearings, but I shall limit myself to the second hearings, which I still remember vividly.

So strong was the interest in these hearings that I wrote for the *Herald Tribune* between 4,000 and 6,000 words each weekday for six weeks running; and hard as this may now be to credit, the *Tribune* published every word I wrote. I hardly recall any longer who the witnesses were, although the Morgan partners were again on the stand for a considerable period, this time without their senior partner. I recall very little, either, of what the witnesses said. What now makes the Nye hearings so instructive, in any case, was the point Senator Nye was trying to prove: that all wars were largely

109

started by arms manufacturers and the bankers serving these "merchants of death" (as arms manufacturers were customarily labeled).

This theory had grown out of the larger theory that arms races give rise to wars. The theory had originated in England in the peculiar climate of the inter-war years, and had been all but patented by the chairman of the Labour Party, George Lansbury. It was quite as responsible for the British failure to rearm in the face of Hitler's threat as the appeasing tendencies of the Tories of the type who cast Winston Churchill into the wilderness for a while. From this English theory, moreover, naturally flowed the primarily American theory adopted and further propagandized by Gerald Nye, that arms races originated because merchants of death encouraged arms races to swell their own profits. But in Nye's case, the particular topic investigated was the wicked way these same merchants of death and their bankers allegedly dragged the United States into the First World War, with the sordid purpose, as almost all liberals believed then, of making sure they would be paid for the arms they had been sloppily permitted to sell to Britain and her allies.

When I came to Washington at the beginning of 1936, I had given no thought at all to matters like these. Life at Harvard had been all books and good times, and there was nothing I experienced in my New York years to make me look outwards, from the city and my own work, to what was happening in the rest of the world. My own work's character then is best suggested by the assignment that earned me my transfer to Washington. This was writing the *Tribune*'s descriptive features for the famous trial of the kidnaper-murderer of the Lindbergh baby. In short I was a *tabula rasa*. I also had deep respect for the senior Washington reporters I first encountered at the Nye hearings, who strongly favored Nye's views. So I was half-convinced by Nye's arguments, and this led to an encounter with my father which piety only partly impels me to set down here; for it also makes several useful points.

My father was a primordial old-fashioned WASP, more a large farmer than a country gentleman, also a businessman, and in his early manhood a leading younger Republican in his own state, Connecticut. Long before he married Theodore Roosevelt's niece, he was one of the first Roosevelt's "young men of our sort" in politics, and he left his party to become a passionate Progressive-Bull Moose partisan in

1912. But his Progressivism gave way to regular Republicanism in the 1920s; and he was as hostile to Franklin Roosevelt and his New Deal as most other WASPs of his kind.

Beginning in the late 1930s, however, my father's sharp hostility to the President and all his works was transmuted into admiring support for every move Roosevelt made to prepare the United States for the world emergency, to aid the Allies, and to deal toughly with the Axis powers. After Pearl Harbor, too, this admiring support of the President never failed throughout the war years, and he thought Roosevelt's death in 1945 a heavy loss to the United States. This by no means implied that my father or the others like him had been converted by the war years to admiration of Roosevelt's domestic policies. The contrary was true, although the passage of time reconciled all but the most bitter and ideological of the President's opponents to a good many of the great New Deal innovations. Above all, however, my father and the others like him had a high opinion of Roosevelt's war leadership, detested those who sniped at the President of the United States in wartime, and mourned his death with almost everyone else in the country and the world.

My father's political history has a good deal of relevance, moreover, to the period of Roosevelt's career I am now attempting to describe; for it reveals a WASP political pattern that was to become important soon after the wind-up of the Nye hearings. The hearings I had covered produced the second Nye neutrality bill. The bill, in turn, led to the encounter with my father which I now want to describe. He was, I should explain, given to decided pungency of language.

"God eternally dammit, Joe," he burst out, "haven't you and your damn-fool Washington friends ever *heard* of this man Hitler? You're beating the drum for that stinker Nye's bill now. But I warn you, within four years Hitler will make you beat the drum a lot harder for the bill's repeal."

In the same turbulent conversation—the talk in our big farmhouse at Avon was often turbulent—my father also predicted that if the Nye bill passed the Congress, the President would want to veto it, for "at least he has some sense about this sort of thing," but the surmise was added that "probably *his* damn-fool friends won't let him do the right thing." Before long, too, the series of forecasts which have now been

111

set down proved correct on all but a single minor count. When the Nye bill passed Congress, the President very much wanted to veto it, and only reluctantly allowed the bill to become law because any other choice would have evoked a liberal storm to end liberal storms. Yet no wonder he was reluctant. All Roosevelt's feelings and ideas from the time of the First World War were already coming to vivid life again, thus proving his good "sense about this sort of thing" as those like my father saw good sense. And nothing could have been more contrary to this brand of good sense than the Nye bill's mandatory embargo on all American arms shipments to any belligerent in any future war, even if one belligerent was the known and unforgiving enemy of this country, and another was this country's long-tested friend.

Again, it was quite true that my Washington friends and I had hardly heard of Adolf Hitler at the time of the talk at Avon. It was then unknown for any reporter working in Washington to write a line about defense or foreign affairs, except in connection with such local circuses as the Nye hearings. For myself and most other reporters in Washington, in fact, the great change only began with the Munich agreement in September 1938. Almost at once, I then began beating my small columnist's drum with great vigor for immediate repeal of the crippling Nye neutrality act; and this was much sooner than the four years my father had predicted—the minor mistake I mentioned earlier.

Nor was the fulfillment of the short-term prophesies I had heard at Avon the only predictive aspect of the encounter there. For the longer term, the episode also predicted the kind of support the President would have to look for, and did look for, as the going got more and more rough in the years preceding Pearl Harbor. Here it is well to remember that even the British Labour Party only ceased to oppose British rearmament after the invasion of Czechoslovakia, when two of my postwar heroes, Clement Attlee and Ernest Bevin, drove George Lansbury from the Labour Party chairmanship on that issue at the party conference of 1939. When Lansbury made another of his speeches about arms races and conscientious opposition to rearmament, Bevin roundly told him everyone was tired of him "carting his conscience from conference to conference." The old man reportedly shed tears when he was repudiated, but he should have saved his tears for what his views and advocacy had done to his country. In Britain, in sum, the left needed much time to

112

face up to the meaning of Hitler; and in the United States, the intellectual liberals were even slower, if anything, than the British left.

Among Roosevelt's other natural supporters, the poor of the big cities were at best indifferent, and the non-WASP middle class tended to be indifferent too, while the Irish generally tended to be actively anti-British. The majority of the Jews took their lead as so often from their large intellectual element, and the Jewish intellectuals in the main were only a little less slow off the mark about Hitler than American liberals of other origins. Hence the principal Northern elements of the New Deal coalition could not be depended upon by Roosevelt for active support along the difficult road that world events forced the President to travel from late 1938 onwards.

It was fortunate the President was so unrelentingly pragmatic, and therefore entirely ready to seek the political help he badly needed in sectors of the electorate where enmity towards him had been the strongest before the danger abroad began to be acute. The South supported him solidly, because Southerners entirely agreed with the view of history's meaning and the way the world works which Roosevelt had espoused in the First World War and never really abandoned. The President's viewpoint, moreover, was essentially the old-fashioned American WASP viewpoint so vociferously expressed during the First World War by Theodore Roosevelt.

Among the Northern WASPs, especially in the Midwest, a good many none the less adopted the brand of isolationism being preached by the young Senator from Ohio, Bob Taft, and further joined the America First Committee when it was organized. Yet a substantial majority of WASPs in the North, including many former Roosevelt-haters, still held their traditional opinions about foreign and defense policy, and they therefore agreed with Roosevelt as heartily and supported him as vigorously as the Southerners. The character of the political line-up in the pre-Pearl Harbor years had its ironic aspects, in truth, and it has therefore been underplayed by most later historians.

These have usually been liberals, and I suspect they hardly like to admit the importance in this line-up of such dubious people as traditional Southerners and old-fashioned WASPs. So far as the historians notice the WASP role, they usually explain it by the supposed Anglophilia of WASP

113

Americans of old stock. But neither Theodore nor Franklin Roosevelt was an Anglophile because they went to English tailors. If I may be honest but perhaps prejudiced, I think the real explanation is that Northern WASPs, like Southern ones, tend to understand that the balance of power is always the mainspring of history—a fact never palatable to American liberal intellectuals.

Belief in the essential importance of the balance of power was certainly the source of the President's extreme disquiet about the events taking place in Europe and across the Pacific in the late 1930s. The second Neutrality Act had been passed and allowed to become law in 1937. But that was also the year of the Marco Polo bridge incident, when the Japanese army, far from content with having seized Manchuria, began the invasion of North China. In that year, too, the Rome-Berlin Axis was plainly taking final shape and had only to be formally announced to the world. Roosevelt therefore tested the water for the first time in October 1937 with his Chicago speech declaring that peace-loving nations must "quarantine" aggressors.

Year by year, for good or ill, the habit had grown on him of dodging all around important and thorny subjects before coming squarely to grips with them in the end; and the quarantine speech was a good sample of this habit. Perhaps because of the careful indirections, the speech received no more than tepid approval, even from those in the press and in politics who would later back Roosevelt's every step towards more rational foreign and defense policies. With his uncanny gift, the President therefore concluded that the time was not ripe, and retreated again into near silence about the situation overseas.

When the quarantine speech was delivered, it should be noted, Roosevelt's power to lead appeared to be gravely undermined. The seedy Texas Congressman Martin Dies managed to secure authority for the House Un-American Activities Committee in 1938, with the unavowed initial aim of going Red-hunting on the fringes of the New Deal. Very naturally, Roosevelt would have liked to stop Dies before he began, for he had an unfailing aversion to Red-hunts wherever conducted. Yet there was nothing he could do about it. Again, he asked for a government reorganization bill that year, with truly bizarre results. Events abroad had at last made the country fascism-conscious, as one may say, and the innocuous and rather badly needed reorganization bill was portrayed by Roosevelt's growing band of political enemies as a first long step towards fascist "authoritarian" ways in the U.S. government. Consequently, the bill barely passed the Senate, and was defeated in the House. Moreover, although the President was already deeply concerned about developments in Europe, not to mention the Far East, he evidently felt he could do no more—in the aftermath of the Munich agreement—than ask for an additional $300 million for the War and Navy Departments.

In November 1938, however, a young Jewish refugee, Herschel Grynszpan, assassinated a secretary of the German Embassy in Paris. Adolf Hitler responded by ordering a Germany-wide pogrom. Thus rather more American eyes at last began to open to the barbarous realities of the world situation. In January 1939, therefore, Roosevelt felt free to order the formation of a strong Atlantic squadron of the U.S. Navy, and to announce a policy of meeting the threat of the fascist powers with "measures short of war but stronger and more effective than mere words." That speech was well received on the whole, but a minor storm blew up before long when an American bomber of the latest design crashed in California. The inquiry revealed that a French military officer had been quietly authorized to go along on the flight, and this led (not incorrectly) to accusations of connivance by the President.

What was really happening was a continual interaction between events abroad and opinion in the United States. As more and more Americans became aware of the gravity of the danger overseas, Roosevelt was more and more free to take actions which he thought appropriate. It was the kind of process he was ideally fitted to gauge with the most minute accuracy, and whenever his freedom of action increased, he always took advantage of this as soon as he thought he had enough support for another step. With great long-term success, he thus went forward in the direction he had always believed in—the direction of the United States at last assuming the full burdens and risks of an active great power with an enormous stake in world developments.

Even so, it was a slow business. March of 1939 brought Hitler's cruel joke on the misguided Neville Chamberlain, when the German army invaded all that remained of Czechoslovakia in open disregard of the Munich agreement. In America, those who saw world problems as the President did could only wring their hands, but Senator Borah of Idaho, the senior Republican member of the Senate Foreign Relations Committee, complacently remarked, "Hitler has taken Europe without firing a shot."

Meanwhile, after casting about for a new move that might be made with safety, Roosevelt could think of nothing more substantial than a message asking both Hitler and Mussolini to pledge to refrain from attacking some thirty-one other nations listed by name. It seemed a silly message at the time, with no threat of force to back it up; and Hitler made the Reichstag laugh by his public mockery of the President. Senator Nye openly rejoiced over the mockery. The President, he said with satisfaction, had "asked for it." Yet hard as it may be to comprehend Roosevelt's fondness for this sort of gesture, he was being shrewder than he looked, as so often; for there is no doubt that the episode of the Roosevelt message and Hitler's response achieved another gain for the President. On the one hand, public opinion again moved a little in the direction the President desired, and on the other, he avoided the fatal appearance of passively resigning himself to what he knew would come in Europe.

So war came relentlessly closer, and not just in Europe. In the Pacific, Japan had proclaimed the formation of the "Greater East Asia Co-Prosperity Sphere"—another way of describing a vast expansion of the Japanese Empire—during the course of 1938. Here it may be well to take brief note of a curious split among Americans which lasted right through the war years. In the war the split manifested itself in the unending argument between those who wanted stronger support for the Pacific theater and General Douglas MacArthur, and those—like the President himself—who wanted to deal first with Hitler. Prewar, getting tough with Japan was even advocated by some otherwise passionate isolationists, while the interventionists almost invariably gave first priority to getting tough with Hitler.

People of the same kidney as those who called for toughness with Japan are now inclined to believe that Roosevelt got the United States into war by crafty design—in fact by taking steps against Japan that would provoke, even invite, the attack on Pearl Harbor. In reality, however, most of the steps against Japan were taken under public pressure, and Roosevelt often resisted this pressure. Thus, nothing was done to interfere with Japan's trade with the United States, most important to the Japanese military as their main source of scrap steel, after Japan seized Hainan Island early in 1939.

Again, in the spring of that year, the Japanese forces in North China blockaded the British and French concessions in Tientsin; and this move led Senator Vandenberg of Michigan, then a leading Republican isolationist, to demand that Roosevelt cancel the U.S.-Japanese trade treaty of 1911. Yet Roosevelt stood pat.

The contrasting half of this pattern was well illustrated when the President asked for repeal of the Nye Neutrality Act, or at least of the clause making an arms embargo mandatory against all belligerents. The Senate Foreign Relations Committee was narrowly divided, and Senator Borah held the key to the outcome. In consequence, after long thrashing about, the President called the relevant leaders of the House and Senate to the White House, and begged them all to give him some cards in his hand with which he could have at least a slim chance of discouraging the European war that was now very near. Secretary of State Cordell Hull then set forth all the reasons for believing war must break out soon. Whereupon Senator Borah, with arrogant bad manners, told Hull to his face that he and his Department knew nothing; that he, Borah, *paid* for better intelligence than Hull got from the American Embassies abroad; and that it was "certain" there would be no war because the British would cave in again before Hitler, as they had done at Munich.

To find out what happened at the White House, I went straight to the Senate Republican leader, Charles McNary of Oregon, who disliked Borah and was infuriated by his behavior to Hull. (You could always tell if Senator McNary was angry, for he wore long starched white shirtcuffs in the style of 1910, and he would shoot the cuffs over and over when really enraged.) Armed with a full account from McNary, I then went to Senator Borah, and asked what was this intelligence he claimed to have paid for. Quite unashamed, he replied that he got all the information he needed by paying a few dollars a year for *The Week,* a most dubious tipster sheet put out by Claud Cockburn, a leading British Communist in those days. Borah, please note, was then supposed to be the Senate's most knowledgeable student of foreign affairs. Such was the situation of the United States on the eve of the Second World War!

So it went thereafter, too, until France had fallen, Britain was in urgent peril, and the United States was thoroughly alarmed at last. Whenever there was an opportunity to move, the President seized it with great firmness. After Hitler invaded Poland and the British and French went to war, the repeal of the embargo provisions of the Neutrality Act was immediately requested again. This time the Congress gave the President what he asked for with minimal resistance; and so supplies of American arms were made immediately available, albeit on a strict "cash and carry" basis, to both France and Britain. Yet it was not until the spring of 1940, after the German onslaught against France had succeeded all too well, that the President even felt free to take in hand the obviously urgent task of putting his own administration on a war footing.

The position at the War Department had long been downright scandalous. The Department was officially responsible not only for the Army but also for most of American air power before the Air Force gained independence. Yet the Secretary of War was the sleazy third-rater Harry Woodring of Kansas. In addition, the Undersecretary, Louis A. Johnson, just as shoddy as his chief though substantially abler and considerably more unscrupulous, was locked in mortal and quite open bureaucratic battle with Woodring, to the point where the two men did not speak to one another. While less publicly shocking, the position at the Navy Department was not vastly better. Yet if Roosevelt had taken corrective action too soon, Woodring and Johnson were just the men to stir up a hornets' nest on Capitol Hill; and for this purpose, since both were vengeful and Johnson was viciously ambitious, these two might well have worked together for the first time.

After the fall of France, however, Roosevelt was emboldened to call in Felix Frankfurter, a leader behind the scenes of the interventionists in Washington although by now a Justice of the Supreme Court. Principally on Frankfurter's recommendation, Roosevelt then asked two of the most conspicuous and highly placed Republican interventionists, Henry L. Stimson, Herbert Hoover's former Secretary of State, and the Chicago publisher and former Theodore Roosevelt Rough Rider, Colonel Frank Knox, to serve as Secretary of War and Secretary of the Navy respectively. Knox thereupon brought in James V. Forrestal, a New York investment banker, to serve as his Undersecretary, while Stimson brought in to the War Department Robert A. Lovett, John J. McCloy, Robert Patterson, and a few more of the same ilk if not quite the same stature. Concurrently,

118

Dean G. Acheson reentered the government after long exile, this time in the State Department. This was when "Dr. Win the War" began to replace "Dr. New Deal."

The change did not please all the New Dealers. Tom Corcoran left the government while Ben Cohen, with different convictions, stayed on to give splendid wartime and postwar service. The new line-up also reduced to near frenzy the more ardent isolationists of all political stripes and all the more partisan Republicans. Yet they were powerless to block Roosevelt's new appointments, primarily because the country was generally enthusiastic about the changes at the War and Navy Departments. So the government pulled itself together for the dread tasks still ahead, and Roosevelt also got another major dividend, in the form of subordinates who would never argue with him about going forward although they often argued about the need to go faster.

Roosevelt took another step forward on his own hook, and this time a long one. He announced as his defense goals a fully motorized and mechanized army and an output of no less than 50,000 combat aircraft a year; and he requested an immediate addition of $700 million to the War Department's funds and another large slice of cash for the Navy.

These actions by the President caught the Republicans between the wind and the water, and even had something to do with the choice of Wendell Willkie as the Presidential nominee of the Republican convention of 1940—because Roosevelt had already set the example of nonpartisanship, and might have won all the anti-isolationist Republican votes if the party's nominee was the wrong sort of man. Willkie's nomination none the less surprised the old-line Republican politicians and a high percentage of the more conventional political wiseacres in Washington. The conventional nominees would have been either Thomas E. Dewey or Robert A. Taft, both of whom had far more first-ballot delegates than Willkie had.

Willkie was essentially a utilities executive and Wall Street lawyer. His two advantages were an odd knack for revivalist oratory, orginally on the subject of free enterprise, which had long impressed the business community, plus foreign policy views that were as near to actively interventionist as those of any politician of that time. The latter asset made Willkie the inevitable candidate of the Republicans who largely shared his opinions on foreign policy. One of the

Republican Party's peculiarities at that period was the unrepresentative character of the isolationist majority of incumbent Republican Senators and Congressmen. These people no doubt represented the powers-that-were in their state organizations. But the Senators and Representatives and the leaders of the state organizations could not get their way when the rank and file felt seriously impelled to express their preferences, as happened at the party's 1940 convention.

Willkie in fact gained his main support from WASPs of much the same sort the President had just brought into the administration. (Several of these latter even meant to vote for Willkie until late in the ensuing campaign.) Fortunately, such men still had very strong leverage in 1940, and many other Republicans thought like them. So the Willkie backers poured into Philadelphia, the convention city, in a passion of fervent support for their man. I had not been warned of the human outpouring, and I incautiously said to a group at the convention that the Willkie movement seemed to come from the "grass roots." With cheerful venom, the reply came from Alice Longworth, "Yes, of course—from the grass roots of ten thousand country clubs." There was something to this put-down, too; yet the enthusiasm for Willkie was all but irresistible; the successes of Adolf Hitler had made both Taft and Dewey look pretty inadequate; and Willkie carried the day on the sixth ballot.

As for the President, those who have dug their way through the enormous archives of the library at Hyde Park—which I cannot claim to have done—now believe that Roosevelt obscurely made up his mind to run for a third term just after the fall of France in June 1940. He loved being President, but he also quite honestly believed the war emergency had made him indispensable, and I for one am sure he was right. At any rate, all the old-line politicians who had never believed a third-term attempt was possible were at length forced to change their minds by Roosevelt's preconvention moves. Since a third-term candidacy had never even been considered before, the President wanted to be drafted; and he chose Chicago as the place for the Democractic convention because the city had become far stronger Roosevelt territory than it had ever been Al Smith territory. As it turned out, the convention was not a joyful occasion, for by no means all those Democrats who went along with the third term were in the least happy about it; and a rebellion very nearly broke out against Roosevelt's choice of Henry A. Wallace for the Vice Presidency. But what mattered was that the country, to its good fortune, now had to choose between Roosevelt and Willkie.

The campaign did not prevent Roosevelt from continuing to go forward in his usual way. The first peacetime draft bill in American history had been jointly offered by Senator Edward Burke, a deeply conservative Nebraska Democrat and an effective anti-Roosevelt leader in the Court fight, and one of the most respected senior Republicans in the House of Representatives, James Wadsworth, a great landowner and country gentleman from upstate New York.

The fact that such a bill was offered at all was a measure of the times, but the fact that it passed was still more remarkable. Roosevelt welcomed the Burke-Wadsworth initiative, gave their bill all the quiet support he could, and then signed it with rejoicing in October.

Late that summer, too, the destroyer-bases deal Roosevelt had contrived with Winston Churchill was boldly announced, with Wendell Willkie's tacit approval. I was actively involved on my own lowly level, for John Foster of the British Embassy had chosen to tell me about the highly secret telegrams from Churchill to Roosevelt begging for the fifty over-age American destroyers then in mothballs. I passed the word on to friends, as was intended; and thus began the public agitation for the transfer of the destroyers to Britain. But the destroyer story has long been a twice-told tale. Only one unknown aspect of it needs to be set down here for the light it casts on Franklin Roosevelt and his longheaded but curious ways.

In brief, I wrote a column that summer, in effect denouncing the President as a mere poltroon for delaying the destroyer transfer so long, whereupon Steve Early called from the White House to congratulate me on a "useful and sensible" contribution. It was useful and sensible, of course, to the extent that it was another morsel of propaganda for Roosevelt taking the road he wanted to travel. The fact that Roosevelt was attacked did not matter a damn to him as long as he was attacked for being too slow to do what he very much wanted to do. No other President in history, as far as I can discover, carried this kind of total preoccupation with results quite so far as Roosevelt, unless it be the American saint with whom none can compare, Abraham Lincoln himself. And Roosevelt was no saint and could be exceedingly touchy about criticism, if the criticism did not serve his own undeclared purposes.

The Presidential election was in full swing when Roosevelt revealed the destroyer-bases deal with the British, and Willkie made no real protest against it. That summer no one, including the President himself, was quite sure whether the British could survive the German air onslaught, which had begun soon after Dunkirk; and while millions in America were watching the British stand up to the German bombers, people's minds were focused on the war situation—which was how sentiment for the draft grew until the Burke-Wadsworth bill passed.

During the autumn, however, apprehension slackened, and the pressure on Willkie from isolationist Republicans correspondingly increased. The Republican candidate was doing rather poorly in any case, and in the end Willkie was harried into beginning a series of attacks on Roosevelt as a man sure to get the country into the war if reelected. This tactic caused Willkie to pick up enough steam to alarm Roosevelt and his advisers. This in turn led to the Roosevelt speeches, late in the campaign, which are now the most criticized he ever made. The key speech was the one in Boston, where he told "fathers and mothers" he was ready to say "again and again and again" that "your boys are not going to be sent into any foreign wars."

I have never been able to decide whether the Boston speech was required by hard-headed political considerations, although it is worth noting that the passionate interventionist Robert E. Sherwood, by 1940 an important Roosevelt speech-drafter, later admitted he had urged the President to make the "no war" promise without hesitations or qualifications. Probably the speech did help Roosevelt significantly with the lower-income groups in the large cities, whose huge majorities for the President played a major role in his fairly easy reelection in November. I daresay it means I have a low character, but the essentially moral criticisms of Roosevelt in this connection have never really convinced me. Anyone who wants to judge campaign speeches by normal standards of morality has insufficient experience of American political history. Furthermore, if Roosevelt deceived the electorate, so did his rival; for Willkie already believed it would be necessary for the United States to go to war, yet denounced Roosevelt for feeling just the same way.

Once the election was safely out of the way, Roosevelt was again free to turn to the urgent business created by the still-deepening world emergency. The Congressional enemies of strong national defense having long since fallen almost entirely silent, what then seemed to be truly enormous increases in the defense appropriations were voted while the election was in progress. A two-ocean navy was requested and authorized before November. In the same period, no less than $17 billion was added to the War and Navy Department appropriations, beginning with the previously noted new money provided after France fell. Roosevelt now proclaimed that the American aim was to serve as a "great arsenal of democracy," and promised half of American war production to Britain. Although that was all very well, an arsenal operating on a cash-and-carry basis is not much use when those in need of arms run out of cash; and a long, carefully factual yet profoundly stirring letter from Winston Churchill gave Roosevelt the news (which he knew well enough already) that the British were nearing the end of their liquid resources, and would soon have no cash to pay for the arms they so urgently needed.

Roosevelt responded with a speech to the country downright dazzling for its shrewd politics in presenting an idea in the right way and for the high-principled statesmanship of the idea presented. Would it not be ridiculous, he inquired in homely tones, to demand cash before lending a garden hose to a neighbor whose house was on fire? Would not any man in his senses simply lend the hose while requesting its return when the fire was put out? This was the way the country learned the basic scheme of the Lend-Lease bill. Inevitably, the isolationists in the Senate, House, and elsewhere raised a fearful cry, and the debate in Congress went past the new year and through part of the winter. Yet early in February the Lend-Lease bill passed by a fair margin, so one more enormous problem had been solved when the need for a solution grew sufficiently urgent.

The time has come to introduce more completely the figure in the drama who was to play an even greater role in the President's last years than Louis Howe had played in the long years of planning and preparation for the Presidency. Howe had faded out of life during Roosevelt's first term, and no one had ever taken his place until Harry Hopkins came along. Of all the men in responsible positions in government whom I have known pretty well—and that means a long list by now—Hopkins always struck me as the most curious human combination. One side of him was all social worker, passionate to relieve human suffering, and exceedingly effective and willing to stop at nothing in meeting great human needs. Yet the other side was an almost anti-social worker. Hopkins was so fond of betting on horse races that he often held WPA staff conferences in the car on the way to the Laurel track in Maryland, and he frequented the races at Belmont whenever he went to New York while the track was open. He also had great liking for worldly and decidedly glittering company, and a particular fondness for young cheerful couples with the careless, easy ways that go with gilded youth. Add that he was a marvelously good talker, both witty and incisive; that he adored pretty women and greatly enjoyed a social drink; and that he cared nothing about money and always appeared to have bought his clothes at a pawnshop. You then have the beginning of a picture of this puzzling and (as I came to believe) altogether memorable and admirable man who literally gave his life for his country as a soldier might in war.

Harry Hopkins had served Roosevelt well throughout the New Deal, and it was probably with the idea of making Hopkins his own political heir that the President finally gave him a Cabinet post as Secretary of Commerce. Before the troubles abroad grew urgent, however, Hopkins succumbed to cancer, and was so close to death that the Roosevelts, with generous warmheartedness, brought him into the White House so they could watch over him. (They did this more than once with old friends in particularly bad health—for example, with Harry Hooker, an old Hyde Park crony of the President who was also close to Eleanor Roosevelt.) To Hopkins, the transfer to the White House then gave a special standing not enjoyed by anyone during the Roosevelt Presidency since the death of Louis Howe. The long enforced rest and good care in the White House restored Hopkins's health to the point where he could work for extended periods like a man possessed, though not without being forced to take to his bed again at intervals and, above all, not without the slow decline of his limited physical reserves, which led to his death after the war was over and his job was done.

I suspect, too, that the transfer to the White House had another significant effect on Hopkins. Since the New Dealers were basically American left-wing intellectuals, a good many of them were far from being interventionists before

Pearl Harbor; and even after the war began, some continued to complain about being supplanted by Dr. Win the War, and to grumble about the war-caused change in the President's priorities. Originally, the evidence suggests that Hopkins had the same feelings as the New Dealers who regarded the danger abroad as an unfortunate interruption of social progress. So it must have been the President who made Hopkins see the world situation in a quite different light. This had happened, however, considerably before the votes were counted in November 1940.

By then, in fact, Harry Hopkins was Franklin Roosevelt's chief confidant about foreign and defense policy. Hopkins was also a preternaturally quick study and had a remarkable knack of rapid, unfailingly sensible judgment; so he came to influence the President far more than anyone else, and to have a unique standing in the U.S. government and later in Britain. It was only logical for the President to choose Hopkins as the man to send to England to establish a closer partnership with the British Prime Minister. Hopkins went in early January 1941, with the private conviction that he would always be needed to serve as an intermediary between two such men as Franklin Roosevelt and Winston Churchill, both of whom preferred holding forth to listening. He changed his mind soon after arriving in London, for he rightly judged that the great Englishman would prove, when it came to the test, one of the very few other men whose flow of talk the great American would find unremittingly delightful and absorbing. Just as important, Churchill and Hopkins struck up a warm friendship, based on intense admiration for each other, which endured until Hopkins's death.

That January, major Anglo-American staff talks between the leaders of the British and American armed services had already begun quietly in Washington; and the staff talks, with all their sequels, plus Hopkins's long sojourn in Britain with all its own significant sequels, were the beginnings of the Anglo-American "common law alliance." The phrase was invented by Robert Sherwood, on the pattern of "common law marriage," and if you take as your model the kind of common law marriage that becomes public knowledge, common law alliance exactly describes the Anglo-American partnership as it was throughout 1941 until Pearl Harbor day. The President himself, who had a special talent for the right gesture at the right time, had called in Wendell Willkie soon after Hopkins went to London. At this meeting Roosevelt proposed what was to become their valuable wartime cooperation; and he had then sent Willkie to London with a personal message to Churchill meant to solemnize the partnership, so to say. The message, which many Englishmen and Americans who lived through that time will still remember with emotion, was a passage from Longfellow written out from memory in Roosevelt's swift, slanting hand:

"Sail on, O Ship of State!
Sail on, O Union, strong and great!
Humanity with all its fears,
With all the hopes of future years,
Is hanging breathless on thy fate!"

After six weeks in Britain, Hopkins returned to the United States as he had gone over, by the just-opened route for big amphibious flying boats, the first air route across the Atlantic and an appalling trip which took five days. As might be expected, he arrived in a state of collapse. The President made him go to bed while he took blood transfusions, yet named him the real administrator of the new Lend-Lease program, although he never had that title. Hopkins now had the most important accumulation of duties and responsibilities in the government after the President himself, but his only office was his White House bedroom and his only desk a card table.

It can be seen, then, why Harry Hopkins deserves a special place in any account of Roosevelt's later life. He not only wielded vast authority, enjoyed the President's absolute confidence, and saw more of him from day to day than any other person—for in this period Eleanor Roosevelt was more and more away from the White House, traveling on the President's business. In addition, as you go up the scale of human quality among the men who served America and Britain so well in the war years, you find that the admiration for Hopkins grows greater and the affection warmer until you reach the top of the scale, with Winston Churchill and General George C. Marshall, a man no sculptor could have portrayed properly except in granite because his judgment and his standards had the integrity of a great block of granite.

Having placed the most important figure in Franklin Roosevelt's later life—unless that rank should be given Mrs.

Rutherfurd after 1941—it is now time to turn to the President's management of his principal task. In that spring of 1941, the most pressing problem was the fearful monthly toll from German submarines of the ships supplying Britain. Partly to relieve the British, who were already in Iceland, but mainly to secure an Atlantic outpost which might be attacked by the Germans, several thousand U.S. Marines were sent to Reykjavik in the late spring. In addition, the Navy was ordered to keep under close surveillance the entire vast area of the Atlantic from the shores of the United States to the 25th parallel, with a large forward extension in the north to include the waters around Iceland. The object was to alert the endangered British convoys to any threat hanging over them. This was stretching "measures short of war" pretty far, but it should also be noted that Hopkins, Secretaries Stimson and Knox, and one or two others whom Roosevelt particularly relied upon at this period were already warning him that direct American intervention in the war might be needed in the end to defeat Hitler's huge armed forces.

At this distance in time, it is exceedingly difficult to reconstruct Roosevelt's own private opinions of the war situation from the fall of France through the summer and autumn of 1940. This is speculation, but I would suggest, first, that between the fall of France and the moment when the RAF gained the upper hand in the air battle over Britain, the President's policy was to wait and see while greatly strengthening U.S. defenses. Charles A. Lindbergh and our serving air officers—the Air Corps was still so bomber-oriented that fighter aircraft were immensely undervalued—had persuaded the American air staff that the RAF had an exceedingly slim chance of standing up to the Luftwaffe. What Roosevelt was waiting to see was whether this intelligence estimate would prove correct. In that event the United States would have been left to stand alone in a hostile world, and as long as this seemed probable or even possible, what the President actually did was the only prudent course. This in turn explains the long delay over the destroyer deal, which was announced only after the RAF had proved its mettle.

Second, it is entirely possible that in October 1940 the President was still managing to persuade himself that direct American participation in the war, at least to the extent of sending large expeditionary forces overseas, could be avoided by the right preventive measures on the right scale.

In this connection it should be remembered that until well into 1941 every letter Churchill wrote to Roosevelt, and every public statement Churchill made, flatly rejected the suggestion that American expeditionary forces would ever be required for victory. "Give us the tools and we'll finish the job," was the Churchill theme. These facts are the context in which to judge the famous Roosevelt campaign speech in Boston.

It seems to me incredible that the President, with all his knowledge and power of down-to-earth judgment, did not realize how events might compel him to do what he so firmly promised he would never do—and to this extent the promise in Boston was unjustified. There can be no doubt, again, that he would always have preferred going to war in deadly earnest to seeing Hitler bring the British to their knees, thus leaving the United States in perilous isolation. But all the evidence suggests that, at a minimum, Roosevelt sincerely *hoped* to keep his Boston promise.

Third, and finally, the evidence is also decisive that this hope, so far as it went, was fading fast by the spring of 1941. Even in the autumn of 1940, as already noted, Secretaries Stimson and Knox were privately warning the President that the war against Hitler could never be won if all the fully mobilized power of the United States was not brought directly to bear. In Britain, too, most people were less buoyant and brave than Winston Churchill, and Hopkins discovered on his first visit that many men at the very top of affairs were self-deludingly convinced that the United States would declare war that spring, and further believed that this was the only real hope. For a while, Hitler's megalomaniac attack on the Soviet Union in June 1941 gave the British and American pessimists a lift, but the German involvement in Russia was at first regarded as no more than a temporary respite. The British and American intelligence services had advance news of the attack, but both at first forecast Hitler's victory in Russia within six weeks or less.

Hopkins was sent off to London again after the attack on Russia, and at Churchill's suggestion he flew on to Moscow in an almost unheated British bomber, thereby nearly killing himself. In Moscow he had the first reasonably frank exchanges with Joseph Stalin that had ever been experienced by any fully independent foreign statesman, and he came back as the first American of any consequence who was prepared to say the Russians might after all hold out for a

128

long time. This was the real beginning of American military aid to the Soviets.

From Moscow, Hopkins flew back to Scotland, where he joined Churchill and sailed aboard that ill-fated battleship *Prince of Wales* to the famous Churchill-Roosevelt conference at sea off Argentia, Newfoundland. The meeting had only two substantive results, the establishment of a close and instant friendship between the two leaders of the West and the proclamation of the Four Freedoms, which had much effect on the world but very little on the war. Greater practical importance in reality attached to the struggle for extension of the Selective Service bill in Washington that summer and fall. If it had not been for the massive moral courage of General Marshall, Roosevelt himself might even have let the draft expire without seeking to renew it; for the feeling had grown strong against it in many quarters.

The truth is that the President was always just a mite fearful of seeming too political to his Chief of Staff, which is easily understandable in view of the aura of perfect uprightness and disinterested patriotism which Marshall always carried with him. While admiring the President greatly as a man and never failing to treat him with the profound respect due his office, Marshall always held aloof enough to be the sole senior officer whom the President never addressed by his first name until the end. After the war I had the rare luck, two or three times, of seeing Marshall in retirement at friends' houses. I confess he looked a bit less like a granite statue when he told me he had always resisted Hopkins's urging to cease being so aloof in his ways, because he feared that if the President called him "George" he would soon be interfering in the Army's internal processes as he did in the Navy's. In sum, Marshall combined great shrewdness with unmatched grandeur, and saw the value of enjoying the President's special respect—a value directly proven in the case of the renewal of the draft.

Luckily, most people in Congress in both parties also regarded George Marshall not just with special respect but with positive awe. Thus Marshall's testimony played quite as large a role as Roosevelt's active though initially reluctant intervention in turning the adverse tide on Capitol Hill. All the same it was a near thing. The extension of Selective Service passed the House by only a single vote.

After the Argentia meeting with Churchill, Roosevelt had greatly stiffened his orders to the Navy's Atlantic patrol vessels. They were now instructed to fire on unauthorized foreign warships and submarines appearing anywhere on the American side of the patrol line Roosevelt had drawn around Iceland and southwards along the 25th parallel. Thus the first American fighting of the Second World War was done by the destroyers *Kearny* and *Reuben James*. That autumn, moreover, Roosevelt requested further radical amendments of the increasingly unneutral Neutrality Act to permit arming U.S. merchantmen and also to permit them to carry munitions and other supplies directly to British ports.

This was as far as anyone could go without an open declaration of war, and Congress only accepted the President's proposal after angry debate. Around the President, none the less, all the advisers he had much use for began continuously pressing him to take the final step, by asking Congress for a declaration of war and thus having the issue out for good and all in a knock-down, drag-out fight with the isolationists. Very luckily, as it turned out, Roosevelt still insisted on waiting until he thought the time was ripe, or else until he had concluded that anything less than a declaration of war would have fatal consequences. Yet he had no notion of how soon this dilemma would be resolved for him, or in what harsh guise the end would come to this time of war–no war.

COMMANDER-IN-CHIEF

The time of war–no war came to an abrupt end, of course, at Pearl Harbor on 7 December 1941. Dispute still simmers about just how that disaster came to happen. The answer is that it happened for reasons at once too simple and too remote from normal American experience to be understood by persons of the sort who have dominated the Pearl Harbor dispute from the beginning. Or this is how it seems to me, after careful analysis of the evidence; and this is how I shall deal with the problem here.

130

To begin with, it is obviously incorrect to suppose that either American diplomacy or American economic sanctions had very much to do with the Japanese decision to make war on the United States. Through a long period of early Japanese military moves on the mainland of Asia, Roosevelt followed the advice of his wise Ambassador in Tokyo, Joseph C. Grew, who urged refraining from provocations in order to give the more moderate Japanese the fullest possible chance to influence national policy. In this period, particularly, the President's relative passivity on the Pacific front was criticized by Senators and others hostile to his policy on the Atlantic front. Over time, however, and at a heightened rate after Grew reported from Tokyo that no more was to be hoped from the moderates because of the impact on Tokyo of Hitler's successes in Europe, the available economic sanctions against Japan were all brought into play.

Both of the raw materials most important to the Japanese war machine, steel scrap and oil, had been embargoed for export well before Pearl Harbor, and all else had been done which might have had a deterrent effect on Tokyo. But everything done was short of war, of course. At the meeting at sea off Newfoundland, Roosevelt rejected Winston Churchill's draft of a proposed joint message to Tokyo because it looked too much like an Anglo-American ultimatum. Meanwhile, in Berlin, the Japanese Ambassador to Germany, Yosuke Matsuoka, had already confided to Hitler that his country would surely go to war with the United States eventually; and this was even before oil exports were embargoed.

What really mattered in this pre-Pearl Harbor period, in any case, was not what the United States and Japan said or even did to one another. What really mattered, rather, was how each country saw its own situation and interpreted the purposes of the other. The American leadership, from the President down, saw the Japanese as irrevocably engaged in a ruthless course of imperial expansion. Some of the main stages of the expansion—first French Indochina and then the Dutch East Indies—were quite accurately foreseen. But a Japanese takeover in Thailand was also expected, although Thailand survived untouched throughout the war. And an attempt on Malaya was considered not probable but merely possible, while Burma was thought likely to be left alone, again incorrectly.

Above all, it never crossed anyone's mind in Washington

131

that the Japanese could even toy with the idea of a direct attack on American positions in the Pacific, or even in the Philippines, where the United States had troops and bases. The foregoing were in fact the main points of a formal estimate by the Army's and Navy's Joint Intelligence Board, which was signed by the Army Chief of Staff and the Chief of Naval Operations, General Marshall and Admiral Harold R. ("Betty") Stark, and submitted to the President on 11 September 1941—or less than three months before Pearl Harbor was attacked. By then, the planning and preliminary preparations for Pearl Harbor were already in progress in Japan.

What had gone wrong? The answer is beyond question. All Americans, markedly including the officers of the armed services, were only too aware of the political limitations on the President's freedom of action. Thus they made the cardinal error of supposing that the Japanese would see their own problems as those problems were seen by American eyes. The officers who prepared the 11 September estimate for the Joint Intelligence Board, and the service chiefs who signed it, and Roosevelt himself who received it, all gloomily foresaw that the President would probably be unable to respond except with gestures if the Japanese seized the rich prizes to be had in Southeast Asia and the Dutch East Indies. Hence they fully expected the Japanese to do what they were obviously able to do with near impunity. But they never expected the Japanese to make the militarily classic move of removing the American threats on their exposed Pacific flank, for they did not regard these threats as real because of the political limitations on the President.

The Japanese, in contrast, from the vantage point of an utterly different training and political system, saw their own situation and American purposes in a way most Americans would have dismissed as insane if they had ever learned of it. There may have been high Japanese officials who had a theoretical grasp of the peculiarities of the American Constitution, but if so they most certainly did not include Gen. Hideki Tojo, the tough militarist who had replaced Prince Fumimaro Konoye as Prime Minister of Japan. With Tojo in power, there was no doubt at all in Tokyo that Japan must move forward from the bases newly acquired in French Indochina to bring the Dutch East Indies (now Indonesia) and further positions in Southeast Asia into the "Co-Prosperity Sphere." Whenever such a move was made, however, this would nakedly expose Japan's Pacific flank.

What came first in the thinking in Washington was apparently not thought about at all in Tokyo. In other words, it occurred to no high Japanese policy-maker then belonging to the inner circle that America's Pacific positions on the Japanese flank were already conveniently neutralized by American domestic politics. Hence a preemptive attack on these American positions, in order to eliminate them, was seen as an unavoidable necessity of the great southwards military movement being eagerly planned and prepared in Tokyo.

In sum, the American and Japanese policy-makers had totally misunderstood each other in every important respect, and from the misunderstanding flowed inescapably what subsequently happened. On the Japanese side, what happened was the successful launching of the surprise attacks on Pearl Harbor, the Philippines, and Malaya. On the American side, what happened was adherence to the smug, unquestioning belief that no such attacks were remotely possible; and this in turn led to the lamentably deficient state of military readiness in all the American positions in the Pacific which enabled the Japanese attacks to succeed all too completely. To the direct connection between the mental and military unpreparedness I can testify myself, from my own experience in Manila on the very eve of Pearl Harbor and the onslaught against the Philippines.

I was serving then as principal staff officer of the American Volunteer Group, or "Flying Tigers," composed of three squadrons of American P-40 planes manned by reserve-officer volunteers from the U.S. Army and Navy, organized by Colonel (later Major General) Claire L. Chennault, and paid for by Chiang Kai-shek's government with U.S. Lend-Lease funds. The AVG had completed its training period at Toungoo, Burma, and was due to go into action in China on 8 December 1941. Although combat was so near, both our P-40s and the machine guns mounted on them were virtually without spare parts, and two or three parts were so short and so critically important that Chennault sent me to Manila to see whether I could get what the AVG most desperately needed from General MacArthur.

As it turned out, nothing was to be had in Manila, but the enduring interest of my trip lay in the fruitless meetings I had there with General MacArthur and members of his staff during the days just before Pearl Harbor and the Philippines were attacked.

MacArthur knew and respected Chennault, which was

133

odd in itself, for MacArthur was very much what used to be called "old army," and the old army despised air officers in general and in particular my chief, who had been a troublemaker while still in the Air Corps. From my column-writing days, he also knew that I had a vague family connection with the President; so the great man received me twice, and allowed himself to unbend a bit each time. Remembering those two exposures to General MacArthur, I later had not the slightest difficulty understanding what I subsequently heard about the follies of the two quarrelsome officers in command at Pearl Harbor, Admiral Husband E. Kimmel and General Walter C. Short.

Total complacency was MacArthur's note. Chennault was already firmly convinced, from the remote vantage point of Burma, that the Japanese would certainly make the great move southwards pretty soon, and he was equally certain they would attack the Philippines when they made their move. Very shortly before the attack came, Chennault even smelled its coming to the day, and ordered me by wire to leave the Philippines by the first plane, and without regard to the state of my mission there. Knowing Chennault's views in this way, I boldly offered MacArthur a thumbnail sketch of my chief's reasoning. The General brushed it aside as not worth listening to, and replied that quite apart from the President's political problems, the Japanese held the name of MacArthur in far too great respect to attack any area under his own protection, such as the Philippines. Pearl Harbor was not even mentioned. In the circumstances, which I must add I have in no way overpainted, I could only thank the General for giving me so much of his time, and bow myself out with suitable respect, thinking—I must confess—that MacArthur might well be more right than Chennault.

I got a different impression that evening, when I was taken to dinner by Chennault's friend, the chief air officer on MacArthur's staff whose name I have now forgotten. He was a pleasant, fairly conventional Air Force Colonel, and he very strongly inclined to the Chennault assessment rather than the MacArthur assessment. To make matters worse, he said, the air arm in the Philippines—in fact his own command—was totally unprepared for war. It was a long dinner, and both of us drank a good deal. In the end, the thought of his own woes led the Colonel to the awful confession that he expected to lose most of his command within moments after

134

a Japanese attack (as actually happened within forty-eight hours); and this confession then reduced the unhappy man to convulsive sobs. It was an odd prelude to the war in the Pacific, which came so soon.

But it was no less odd than what happened the next day, when Chennault's telegram came, and I was busy packing and getting a reservation on the plane to Hong Kong. I had been asked to dinner that evening—the evening before Pearl Harbor Day—by an old Philadelphia friend, Warwick Scott. He had joined up long before, had got a commission in the Navy, and had been ordered to the Philippines, where he was to meet death in Manila Bay only a little later. He took me to the Manila officers' club, a big, rather luxurious, and noisy place, where we talked of home and old friends with some difficulty, while a belly dancer performed for other diners who felt less exiled!

If you reflect on these experiences of mine in Manila, and remember that one of the really brilliant American general officers, Douglas MacArthur, was in virtually sole command in the Philippines, you can find nothing in the least surprising in what happened at Pearl Harbor. Admiral Kimmel and General Short were far less able and imaginative men than MacArthur. Furthermore, command at Pearl Harbor was shared between these two who were hardly on speaking terms. No wonder the official war warning sent by Admiral Stark to the Navy's establishments in the Pacific was not seriously attended to by Kimmel. MacArthur must certainly have known of this war warning when he received me the second time, yet he disregarded it completely because he did not believe it—and, God knows, his command in the Philippines was sadly unready for what followed.

Admiral Kimmel unquestionably shared General MacArthur's opinion, for late in November his staff prepared a broad assessment which flatly stated that there was "no probability" of a Japanese attack on the Hawaiian islands. As for the vile suggestion that Roosevelt wanted the attack on Pearl Harbor in order to be able to declare war, I have no doubt that he would have liked to declare war even before Pearl Harbor, although perhaps not on Japan as well as Germany, and that he would have done so, too, if he had not been prevented by his sense of the politically possible. But it is a long way from this to a President positively desiring a national disaster to sweep away all opposition to a declaration of war, and vile is the precise adjective for those who have claimed that such a thought even entered Roosevelt's mind.

In truth, the evidence suggests that the President was just as wrong in his expectations of Japanese action as everyone else of real consequence. The late November assessment by Admiral Kimmel's staff had placed the bulk of the Japanese war fleet at Kure and Sasebo, although the great force destined for use against Pearl Harbor was already at sea. A day before the curtain went up, moreover, Washington got word that the Japanese naval force destined for Malaya had actually been sighted at sea, and this was promptly and quite wrongly interpreted as meaning that Thailand was about to be attacked. At 9:30 in the evening before Pearl Harbor, the code breakers then unraveled the last Japanese cable sent to the Ambassador in Washington, Kichisaburo Nomura. The text was carried immediately to the White House and handed to the President, who was in his study with Harry Hopkins. He read the Japanese cable carefully, and handed it to Hopkins with the comment "This means war."

Even then, however, the President was apparently convinced that the war would be in Southeast Asia, leaving American areas untouched. When the President sought to talk on the telephone with Admiral Stark, the Chief of Naval Operations was at the theater, and Roosevelt decided it was unnecessary to cause a stir by paging him—which he would never have hesitated to do if he had expected any American positions to be directly attacked.

The first word reached the President, in fact, only at 1:40 p.m. on Pearl Harbor Day, when Secretary Knox telephoned from the Navy Department to say that a radio signal from Honolulu had been picked up, in which Admiral Kimmel advised all naval stations of an air raid there, and added bleakly, "This is no drill." Hopkins still thought there must be some mistake, but the President was wiser now, and thought the report probably true. He therefore called to warn Secretary of State Cordell Hull, who was about to have his last meeting with Ambassador Nomura and the Japanese special negotiator, Saburo Kurusu.

At 2:28 Admiral Stark telephoned the White House with word that the attack on Pearl Harbor was only too real, and had been very severe. The President thereupon called the first wartime meeting of government leaders—the Secretar-

136

ies of State, War, and Navy (Hull, Stimson, and Knox)—and the two service chiefs, Marshall and Stark. At this meeting, the President took the incoming telephone calls himself, and was thus the first to hear the more and more terrible reports of damage to the fleet at Pearl Harbor. And so the United States was at war at last, although the President only asked the Congress for a formal declaration of war the next day, when he appeared in person at the Capitol before a joint session of the House and Senate.

By then, as nearly as I can calculate, I had caught the last normal plane to leave Manila before the war and was making the last routine commercial landing in Hong Kong until some four years later. Thus, I cannot speak firsthand of what happened in Washington on Pearl Harbor Day. Yet I think it is still worth telling two stories of that day's events which came to me on the best authority when I went back to Washington for short intervals in wartime. The first story came from Justice Frankfurter, who had it from Secretary Stimson. He passed it on to me in late 1942, when I got home from wartime internment in Hong Kong thanks to a Japanese-American exchange of internees.

As Justice Frankfurter told the story, Admiral Stark had shown increasing agitation at the White House meeting, and had even dropped a tear or two, as one report after another came in, all telling of great capital ships with many men aboard sent to the bottom by bombs from Japanese airplanes. After the meeting, the President asked Secretary Stimson to stay behind for a moment, only to remark to him when they were alone that he now knew at last why Admiral Stark's nickname was "Betty." "I suppose," said the President, "it was either that or Emily, and Betty seemed more appropriate." Thus the President's decision to replace his Chief of Naval Operations with the limitlessly tough Admiral Ernest J. King must be assumed to have been quietly taken at that meeting on Pearl Harbor Day. Shortly thereafter Stark went to London as chief of the Naval Liaison Mission.

As for the second story, I heard it from the President himself in 1943, when I returned from China more briefly for a second visit to Washington, in order to be present on the fringes of the Trident Conference, because great decisions about China policy were to be reached. I was asked to dinner at the White House during this visit, and as this was the last time I ever saw Franklin Roosevelt face to face, I ought to remember the occasion with emotion. I am afraid, however, that I chiefly remember the dinner's comic side.

Mrs. Roosevelt was away on still another wartime trip, and those the President had chosen to spend the evening with him were Crown Princess Martha of Norway, with whom he had an extremely mild flirtation, two relations of the Crown Princess, the Grand Duchess of Luxembourg and an impoverished cousin who made hats, plus Alexander Woollcott, Harry Hopkins and his wife Louise (who had come to live with Hopkins in the White House after they got married), and finally myself. The President did his best to make his party "go," offering an extra round of his special cocktails before dinner while talking gaily of their allegedly fearsome strength, and then making great efforts to get his other guests to talk after the move was made to a reduced table in the cavernous but beautiful state dining room. First Woollcott, a famous talker, was given the floor; Hopkins followed; and at last my turn came too. But it was no use. The three royal ladies heard us with the obvious boredom and impatience of people watching the acrobats perform while waiting for the star attraction in an old-fashioned vaudeville. When I was asked to tell a little about China, I positively feared I should soon hear a snore, so I fell silent the moment I could do so without being rude. Having done all he could to avoid it, the President then had to talk himself.

He was obviously determined not to talk about the war, of which he no doubt had quite enough during his long and grueling working days, so he mainly took refuge in telling antiquated stories of the New York past, of the sort that used to go around the men's clubs when people still believed a real war was unthinkable. Only once did the President come near to talking about the war. To the obvious delight of the royal ladies, he introduced this part of the conversation with a question asked in a way that anticipated mystification. "Do you know," he said, "what was the first order I issued following the first meeting after Pearl Harbor here at the White House?" All professed the expected mystification, although I guessed from their faces that Harry and Louise Hopkins had heard this story at least once before. "Well, then," said the President, "my first order forbade the construction of a single wartime temporary building in the whole city of Washington without my own initials on the plans and specifications."

The royal ladies now looked bewildered, and so did I. Of course, I had observed the hideous, jerry-built temporary buildings now covering the remaining open spaces of the nation's capital like a particularly nasty attack of architectural eczema, but even I could not figure out the reason for the President's order. For the royal ladies, he then explained what temporary buildings were; he deplored the resulting ugliness of the city; and he finally pointed out that the temporary buildings from the First World War, being sturdily constructed of steel and concrete, had never been permitted to go out of use. So he went on to his story's climax, which concerned the visit of the Chief of Army Engineers, a very great man in those days, who brought the first new temporary buildings' plans and specifications to the White House for the President to initial as ordered. The President took the plans and specifications from the already angry General, who resented interference; he glanced at them briefly; and he tore them to bits before the General's very eyes. (He imitated his own action, grinning with delight, his cigarette cocked in his holder as usual.) The General, red with fury, managed to control himself enough to say with great hauteur, "May I inquire, Mr. President, why you have torn up these plans and specifications, which exactly followed the precedents of the First World War?"

Again, the President mimicked his own past gesture, this time making a stabbing motion towards a window with his cigarette holder. "General," he quoted himself as saying, "you just go to that window and tell me whether the Navy and Munitions Buildings are still there." These buildings, long used by the War and Navy Departments, were in fact out of sight from the Oval Office, but he had evidently correctly calculated what the increasingly furious General would say. His response was to assert indignantly that the two buildings still stood on the Mall, which they had been disfiguring by then for nearly a quarter century. Again the President quoted himself, this time speaking in a tone of triumph: "That's just what I mean, General. *Not temporary*. Now you go right back to your office and design me some really temporary buildings, guaranteed to fall down within seven years; for this war can't possibly last that long. Then I'll initial any plans you bring me with great pleasure. But remember, seven years!"

As it turned out, much costly and wasteful propping and patching made the temporary buildings from the Second

World War last much more than seven years. They were only swept away, in fact, in President Kennedy's time, when the Navy and Munitions Buildings were swept away too on the same tide of delight in the renewed beauty of the capital city. Yet none of this could imaginably have happened without that order of Franklin Roosevelt's and those supplementary instructions he gave the infuriated Chief of Engineers.

I have included both stories here, partly from a desire to make my own small but fresh contribution to the history of Roosevelt as a war President, but above all because these stories are not as trivial as they seem, since they tell much about Roosevelt as a war leader. The second story, to begin with, reveals one of his minor, hardly known, yet most endearing traits. In some sense, he regarded Washington and its environs as the President's very own, in the manner of the great English 18th-century landowners who rebuilt whole countrysides to improve the prospect from their rural palaces. Long before the war, he had fought hard for the Jefferson Memorial; and this horrified his more progressive advisers, who naturally held theories borrowed from the Bauhaus in the 1930s and hated the Jefferson Memorial accordingly. I always wondered why the Memorial meant so much to Roosevelt until I dined one night with President Kennedy and chanced to note how perfectly the marble neo-Greek structure closed the vista from the White House, in the exact manner of an English grandee's "folly" temple closing the main vista through his park. By the same token, one of Roosevelt's first thoughts after the Pearl Harbor meeting at the White House was about whether he, as war President, would leave Washington to his successors irremediably disfigured by wartime scars.

In addition, this story of how the new temporary buildings were required to fall down in seven years is the best proof I know of the enormous value of simple experience in government. The President had seen the wrong thing happen before, and he knew just how to prevent it from happening again. But both stories, it seems to me, also prove another larger point. Franklin Roosevelt could never have been a great war President, as I think he was, without his total imperturbability and firm belief that any disaster could only be temporary, which quite largely derived from his never-shaken Christian faith. In bad times, as his wife later wrote, he literally and humbly believed God was with him and would not desert him. And why not, for his chief adversary

140

as he saw it, was one of the truly wicked men of the 20th century, and who can say Roosevelt was not fighting for good against evil?

So he was debonair with Secretary Stimson about Stark, as well as a bit malicious about the Admiral whose fits of near cowardice during the negotiation of the destroyer-bases deal the President no doubt recalled with distaste. He was debonair enough again to take time off to safeguard Washington's future beauty on the very day of Pearl Harbor (if he did not alter the timing to improve this story; for he was always improving his stories). And once again, he was debonair in the spring of 1943, when the war's great tides were not yet flowing his way, and he gave his little party and kept his royal ladies happy with old stories until they rose to say goodnight.

Few any longer remember precisely the stages of Roosevelt's career before he reached the White House, or the chronology and the achievements of the New Deal years. Hence it has seemed best to deal with these matters on what may be called a summary-historical system. But even those born after the fighting ended still remember that the Second World War was won by Britain, the United States, and their allies. Hence I shall not deal hereafter with the grand stages of the war, stirring and glorious as these sometimes were; nor shall I recount the conferences of the war leaders, or try to follow their exchanges between conferences.

This is, or is intended to be, a somewhat personal memoir of Franklin Roosevelt. His most remarkable contribution as a war leader was the way his boldness and his craft, his never-failing sense of political realities and his far-sighted statesmanship finally brought the great majority of Americans to acknowledge the need for the United States to play a new and larger role in the world. A great President, in my opinion, is above all a great teacher of his people; and all of us still repeat, albeit unknowingly, the lessons we have learned from each of our great Presidents from George Washington onwards. In the crisis of the Second World War, Roosevelt's teaching was made easier by the enemies of the United States. But only consider what the outcome might have been with a run-of-the-mill President—average timorous, average maladroit, average self-interested, average unimaginative—in the place that Roosevelt filled so well! It is a

141

thought to make one's blood run cold, and to fill one with gratitude to Providence for giving the country Franklin Roosevelt when the need was so great and so urgent.

This being said, what further needs saying about Roosevelt as war President concerns only the way he discharged his dreadful burden of wartime responsibilities, the faults he showed in doing this, and the virtues which far outweighed the faults. His conduct of the war had three dominating themes: his world partnership with Winston Churchill; his White House partnership with Harry Hopkins; and his trust in the two service chiefs he had chosen for wartime, General Marshall and Admiral King.

So much has been written already about the Churchill-Roosevelt partnership that it will suffice to describe how this took the final shape which it fortunately maintained until the President's death. Only days after Pearl Harbor, Winston Churchill, Lord Beaverbrook, and a selection of British military leaders steamed out of the Clyde on a new warship, *Duke of York*, and made the slow voyage in North Atlantic winter weather to see the President in Washington. At the White House, the British Prime Minister, of course, had the best bedroom. As Robert E. Sherwood recorded in his fine *Roosevelt and Hopkins*, the food at the White House improved noticeably in Churchill's honor, and drink flowed more freely. Churchill's map room was installed across the hall from his bedroom, and since he used his bedroom as his Washington office a novel traffic of British Embassy personnel and staff officers now enlivened the normally quiet family floor of the old house—whence James and Dolley Madison fled the British in the War of 1812.

What really mattered for the future, however, was that the British and American war leaders now progressed from mutual liking and respect to warm intimacy. Churchill stayed no less than two weeks at the White House, for there was much to do. Daily he and the President spent hours together, often alone with Hopkins; almost daily they lunched together alone with Hopkins; and in the evening, there were little parties, for which Roosevelt would perform his ritual of making the cocktails himself, and the Prime Minister would then wheel the President to the dinner table in his light, mobile chair. Nor was that all. Going to bed early and waking early was Roosevelt's habit, rigidly adhered to in normal times; but Churchill's habit was to do the opposite, and temptation led Roosevelt to alter his usually sacred schedule. He was tempted because he could not bear to miss the late evening talk between Hopkins, so incisive and so laconic, and Churchill, with his grander periods, his flashes of wit, and his sudden pounces on the past to illuminate the present.

I do not wish to be sentimental; yet I find it profoundly moving to think of the reunion of these men, no longer young, one half-paralyzed and one, Hopkins, already harboring a mortal disease, whose shoulders none the less so strongly bore so much of the burden of the future. In background and outlook each differed from the others. Roosevelt and Churchill in particular were of very different natures, as Sir Isaiah Berlin has pointed out. Churchill, with his enormous historical reading and his position as leader of an Empire on its downward slope, was in essence an historical pessimist with too much heart and courage to accept defeat; whereas Roosevelt, with his provincial formation, his far narrower and more specialized historical knowledge, and his old-fashioned religious faith, was an unquenchable optimist, whose optimism might even have been dangerous if it had not been tempered by his enormous political experience and his almost unfailing political realism.

No wonder, then, that each of these two sometimes doubted the judgment of the other, Churchill thinking Roosevelt too superficial and naively hopeful, Roosevelt thinking Churchill too influenced by the wicked ways of the older world he came from and spoke for. The real wonder is that two great leaders with such immense power and such strong egos should have enjoyed one another so much in these weeks they had together in Washington in the grim time after Pearl Harbor.

Churchill came to Washington deeply afraid that Roosevelt might give total priority to defeating the Japanese, as would certainly have seemed politically necessary to a President of smaller stature. Instead, Roosevelt entirely understood that by defeating Adolf Hitler, Japan would also be defeated, whereas defeating Japan and its ramshackle new empire would still leave Hitler in control of most of Europe. Hopkins and the American Chiefs of Staff also saw the priorities in the same way, so the talks in Washington got down to detailed business without long abstract arguments. Many decisions of great future import were therefore taken—for example, raising the targets of all forms of American munitions production to really astronomical levels, which at first seemed impossibly unpractical to Winston Churchill. (The British in Washington had even grumbled earlier about the creation of a large American army, fearing competition for what they believed was a limited supply of American arms.)

Yet the most far-reaching result of this remarkable Washington reunion of the two allies was the unspoken decision of Roosevelt and Churchill to be close friends forever after. The friendship was the cornerstone of the Western alliance throughout the war, never interrupted by the differences their correspondence reveals, or dimmed by any of the subsequent meetings. This even held true at Teheran, where Churchill must have been inwardly wounded by his friend's somewhat sly efforts to be first with Stalin, which Roosevelt made in the naive belief that he, the American liberal, could work more successfully with the Russian Communist dictator than could Churchill, the British Tory imperialist. Despite such little rubs, this was a partnership of the war leaders of two great nations like no other one can think of in history.

Of the relationship between Roosevelt and the American military leaders, not a great deal needs to be said. He had chosen the two service chiefs himself. The circumstances behind the choice of Ernest J. King as Chief of Naval Operations have already been touched upon. Roosevelt wanted a fighting admiral—and he got one. General Marshall had been brought to Washington much earlier, and the story of his appointment is instructive.

The U.S. Army of the late 1920s and most of the 1930s was not only tiny and almost wholly without modern equipment, it was also almost completely dominated by an antiquated elite of cavalrymen, whose boots (always from Peel in London) shone splendidly, in contrast to their intellects, which did not. Roosevelt may not have understood this curious situation in detail, but he plainly saw something was wrong, and he therefore made a solemn journey to Walter Reed Hospital, where the American hero of the First World War, General John J. Pershing, lived in his last years. From his hospital room, Pershing nominated Marshall to lead the army through the coming time of danger. Pershing wanted Marshall because he was the outstanding officer of the subordinate elite the cavalrymen had been keeping down, namely the men who had done well in the higher officers' schools Pershing had established after the First World War. Thus the choice of Marshall to lead the Army meant the vital replacement of its obsolete elite with this new elite—a process never unattended by heartbreak.

Although Marshall was then a very junior officer by Army standards, and General Malin Craig, the preceding Chief of Staff, was a cavalryman born and bred, Craig nobly though sadly approved Marshall as the best man for bad times. This choice of Marshall always thereafter gave the President pride and satisfaction; and he generally followed a hands-off policy as far as the Army's inner processes went. In the whole course of the war, in fact, the President made only two decisions on his own concerning the higher command and management of the Army.

The first was the choice of Dwight D. Eisenhower as the best man to lead the Western allies across the Normandy beaches to the conquest of most of Europe. It was a hard choice, for although Eisenhower was Marshall's protégé, the Chief of Staff would have liked to assume command in the field for the war's grand finale. The place was offered him by the President, and he was overjoyed. In the upshot, however, General Marshall, the great organizer of victory and personal exemplar of a generation of American fighting men, was found to be indispensable in Washington, so the offer was lamely withdrawn and Eisenhower was named. Marshall, with his perfect disinterestedness and sole care for his country, made no audible murmur of discontent.

As for Roosevelt's only other significant decision concerning the Army's higher command, it was one that is now most unfashionable. This was the recall of General Joseph W. Stilwell, Marshall's choice to command the China-Burma-India Theater. In the eyes of all right-thinking American liberals today General Stilwell was a Good Thing because he hated Generalissimo Chiang Kai-shek, well known to be a Bad Thing. Indeed he did hate Chiang. He had detested the Chinese leader since his prewar service in China in the military intelligence; and he came to hate him so violently that he could not resist publicly inflicting pain and humiliation on this Chinese leader with whom he was supposed to work in harness for the common good. This can be easily seen by reading the extremely unpleasant poem General Stilwell himself wrote in premature triumph about an incident in the summer of 1944, which in fact produced the

Generalissimo's request for Stilwell's recall. Roosevelt was himself extremely conscious of being a chief of state, and in his eyes extreme hatred for an allied chief of state was far from a recommendation for a theater commander. Thus, Roosevelt finally acceded to Chiang Kai-shek's request, thereby temporarily displeasing General Marshall very deeply. Over all, none the less, Marshall always considered Roosevelt a "great war President," or so he told me—although I suspect that this great soldier, who had the horror of politics and politicians of the old-style American army officers, always found Roosevelt less appealing as a man than Hopkins, with his astonishing courage in illness and his devil-take-you way of discussing policy choices.

What may be called the civilian side of the war government in Washington was led by the President himself, with Hopkins as his chief adviser and liaison man. In the White House another figure of real consequence was added soon after Pearl Harbor, when Roosevelt recruited James F. Byrnes to serve as Director of Economic Stabilization. Byrnes, who had gone from the Senate to the Supreme Court, willingly left the high bench at Roosevelt's request; and once in his office in the East Wing, he spared Roosevelt much of the enormous burden of managing wartime economic problems. Another enormous burden was also transferred when Hopkins asked the President to name Edward R. Stettinius as Lend-Lease Administrator. Thus Roosevelt and Hopkins in effect reserved themselves for foreign policy, higher defense policy, and the complex relations with Britain, the Soviet Union, and the other allies, plus domestic politics, always unavoidable. Every ounce of final authority was always in the President's hands, but it should be noted that Hopkins not only served as Roosevelt's most important adviser; in a rather odd way, he was also Roosevelt's intermittent interpreter to the rest of the world. The President had a way of being fairly Delphic when plain speaking was likely to be unwelcome; but when he did not make his wishes entirely clear, he always knew that Hopkins could be trusted to explain what he wanted done with extreme clarity and forthrightness.

Something more should be said, too, about the way foreign policy was handled, if only because Americans have such short historical memories. When President Kennedy and his foreign policy adviser, McGeorge Bundy, made foreign policy in the White House without much reference to

146

the State Department or the Secretary of State, Dean Rusk, and again when President Nixon and his adviser, Dr. Henry A. Kissinger, carried the same process even further as long as William Rogers was Secretary of State, the system was both times widely described as improper and unprecedented. But the same system had prevailed under other strong Presidents before Franklin D. Roosevelt's time. Certainly, well before Pearl Harbor, Roosevelt and Hopkins had become the sole real makers of foreign policy. Secretary Hull remained in office through much of the war and was treated with outward respect, but necessary business with the State Department was none the less mainly transacted through the Undersecretary, Sumner Welles, a friend of the President's youth and a man whose way of doing business was closer to the ways of Roosevelt and Hopkins.

This pattern was finally broken, however, by one of the ugliest of those episodes of personal spite which, alas, were not unknown in wartime Washington, with its many rivalries and its recurrent outbursts in Congress of the meanest isolationist resentment. Welles was at a minimum bisexual, and when he had a few drinks he was capable of giving the homosexual side of his nature a freer rein than was entirely wise in a man in his position. Somewhat ludicrously and most unfortunately, this had happened on Speaker William Bankhead's funeral train, and a report of the incident was made to the railroad officials.

Nothing further happened at the time, but much later the report in question was somehow obtained by William C. Bullitt, Roosevelt's former Ambassador to Moscow and then Paris. Bullitt was another friend of the President's younger days, who hated Welles and blackly envied the latter's more frequent wartime access to Roosevelt and Hopkins. He was a dangerous hater too, and he circulated the report on Welles to members of the Senate with many a pious protestation about his patriotic motives in doing so. This lighted partisan fires, and Secretary Hull, who had also come to hate Welles, did nothing to put them out. Hence Welles finally resigned to avoid a public scandal, and was then replaced as Undersecretary by the transfer of Stettinius from the Lend-Lease Administration.

The sad little story would have no place in this memoir if it did not have to be set down in order to make its sequel comprehensible. The sequel began when Bullitt oiled his way back into Roosevelt's presence, with results which speak volumes about the President's personal viewpoint and standards of behavior. Looking hard at his former friend, Roosevelt told Bullitt to his face that he wished to pass on to him a parable about two men who successively but almost simultaneously requested admission at Heaven's Judgment Seat. The first man had a foolish weakness, which the second man had used to destroy him on this weary earth. But at the Judgment Seat the weakness was forgiven and he was told to enter in; whereas the second man, who had intentionally destroyed another, was refused permission to pass through the gate. In her subsequent memoirs, Mrs. Roosevelt gave an account of this singular conversation with obvious and justifiable pride. She named no names, but the identifications here offered are entirely beyond question. The parable in turn explains how the President, to whom Bullitt had toadied for so long, came to be abruptly added to the ever-lengthening Bullitt hatred-list.

But I have got too far from the way foreign policy was made in wartime. To complete that story, Hull resigned for genuine reasons of health in November 1944, and Roosevelt then promoted Stettinius to the Secretaryship, undoubtedly because he was a man who would be (and was) content to make no contribution of his own beyond installing telephones of several different colors on the desks of all the more important State Department officers. The young Charles E. Bohlen, whom Hopkins had found to act as Roosevelt's chief personal expert on Soviet affairs, had far more weight at the White House than the Secretary he officially served under; and this first great upward step in Bohlen's subsequent great career is another indication of the way the President handled big foreign policy decisions.

To complete this part of the story, Harry Hopkins's place as the President's omnipresent and indispensable junior partner was distinctly diminished after their return from the Cairo and Teheran conferences shortly before Christmas 1943. Hopkins had married the beautiful Louise Macy in July 1942, the wedding having taken place in the White House, with the President acting as his friend's best man. Hopkins's wife had then moved into the White House with him, where Diana Hopkins, Harry Hopkins's daughter by his earlier marriage, had already been living ever since her father had settled in at the combined insistence of both Roosevelts. Before Hopkins's marriage, he had even asked Mrs. Roosevelt to bring up Diana herself if anything should happen to him, and she had readily promised to do this, even assuring Hopkins, who had never saved a nickel, that a little money would be available to take care of Diana when her education was completed. Now, both the President and his wife were also warmly welcoming to the new Mrs. Hopkins, but it would have been unnatural if Louise Hopkins had not ended by wanting a house of her own. The new house had finally been secured, and Harry Hopkins joined his wife there immediately when he got home from Teheran.

Hopkins undoubtedly foresaw that his role as the President's junior partner would be lessened by this physical separation, for nothing could quite replace the innumerable daily contacts between the two men which had automatically resulted from Hopkins's constant presence under the President's own roof. Perhaps he was even willing that this should happen, for his always frail health was now beginning to break down much more often and more seriously under the daily strain and burden of the war; and besides moving to a house of his own, he was more and more forced to spend a great deal of time in bed.

Roosevelt did not take Hopkins along to the second Quebec Conference in September 1944, although he had been the strongest American presence, after the President himself, and sometimes General Marshall, at every preceding great wartime and prewar meeting of leaders. By this time, Roosevelt's own vitality—formerly unquenchable—had at last begun to flicker under the same strain that was all but killing Hopkins before his friend's eyes. At Quebec the President was already bone-tired; and this, plus the want of counsel from Hopkins, always tough-minded, no doubt led to Roosevelt's two most surprising, if not most damaging, errors as war President. One was putting his name to the favorite plan of his friend and Secretary of the Treasury, Henry Morgenthau, Jr., for turning the whole of conquered Germany into a near goat pasture. It was a mistake he always regretted and further ignored after the Quebec meeting. The other mistake was putting his name to a telegram to Generalissimo Chiang Kai-shek couched in terms most uncharacteristically brutal, for Roosevelt did not favor failures of good manners in messages to other chiefs of state. It was this telegram which then precipitated the incident which in turn led Chiang Kai-shek to request the recall of General Joseph W. Stilwell.

As to Roosevelt's wartime errors with more lasting effects, only two are so significant that they cannot be wholly passed over. The first was the declaration at Casablanca that nothing less would be accepted than the unconditional surrender of the enemy powers. It is generally acknowledged now that insistence on an enemy's unconditional surrender is never justified. It is not easy to judge whether the unconditional surrender demand prolonged the European fighting by discouraging other German leaders from doing business with the Western allies behind the back of Adolf Hitler. It is certainly true, however, that the theme of unconditional surrender, which President Truman at first felt he had to insist upon after his predecessor's death, came close to producing a Japanese-American bloodbath in 1945 on a scale hideously surpassing the dreadful human losses that had gone before. This climactic bloodbath was avoided, in fact, only because President Truman finally changed his mind enough to indicate that even after Japan had surrendered, the Emperor Hirohito might remain on his ancestors' throne. As a result, all sorts of self-appointed guardians of American public virtue were loudly horrified by the maintenance of "the Emperor system."

Throughout the war, unfortunately, an error far worse than the unconditional surrender demand was also committed—or so I believe—in Roosevelt's and Hopkins's dealings with Joseph Stalin. I believe this simply because I cannot believe that all of Eastern Europe need have been reduced to a series of unhappy provinces of the new Soviet Empire if the American war leaders had been a good deal more tough with Stalin. In this matter Winston Churchill was considerably more far-sighted than his partners in Washington. Yet even the actions of such men as Roosevelt and Hopkins must always be judged in the context of the times, and it must be noted that the context of the times was wholly unfavorable to real toughness.

For one thing, almost no Americans came out of the 1930s with the remotest inkling of the character of Stalin and of the monstrous system he had created for ruling his great country. The principal instruments of misinformation were people like the remarkably intelligent but sadly silly English intellectuals, Beatrice and Sidney Webb. To read their book on Russia today, while recalling the realities in the workers' paradise they described, comes close to being an emetic experience. They had plenty of American counterparts too, albeit of somewhat less eminence; and worst of all, in the sense of most damaging, the American press was on average grossly misleading about the Soviet Union until well after the Second World War was over.

The authority on Soviet affairs was universally held to be the *New York Times* correspondent in Moscow, Walter Duranty, who received two Pulitzer prizes for his work in Russia. The nature of his reporting can be gauged by what happened in the case of the dire, Stalin-induced famine in the Ukraine in the early 1930s. William Stoneman, then in Moscow for the old *Chicago Daily News*, had brilliantly contrived to get to the Ukraine and to send out an accurate account of the horrors of this famine in which five million people were lost. The Soviet authorities thereupon gave Duranty all facilities to go to the Ukraine himself, whence he sent back word that there were no real signs of horrors. The Duranty cover-up, for that was what it was, also continued thereafter; and no one of consequence told the terrible truth.

This being the climate in the United States, Roosevelt and Hopkins would have had to be very different men to make boldly formed judgments of the Soviet system and Stalin's doings and purposes in defiance of almost everyone else who was then thought to be enlightened. They had neither Churchill's strong sense of history as an always perilous process, nor his pessimism about the aims of most great powers and their ways of dealing with each other. They had a State Department by no means devoid of men conservative enough to be suspicious of the Soviets, but with almost no one who truly *knew* the Soviet Union except for two men comparatively junior, the already mentioned Bohlen and his partner of those days, George F. Kennan. The horror of politics felt by General Marshall and a good many men on his staff also played a role, for it was carried to the point of virtually ignoring the Clausewitz rule that war ought to be an extension of politics by "other means." Add, finally, that both the American military and civilian leaders went on much too long fearing that the Soviets would take the first opportunity to leave the war, which made blackmail by Stalin all too easy. Then the American wartime dealings with the Soviets are at least understandable.

Charles Bohlen, another old friend I am proud to claim, used to tell me that if the President had lived longer, the dealings with the Soviets in his fourth term in office would have largely counterbalanced his wartime dealings with them. It is certainly true that following the Yalta Conference

151

in February 1945, Roosevelt's messages to Stalin grew more stern in tone. Nor is this surprising, for commitments Stalin had made to Roosevelt were being flatly disregarded. Yet I cannot help thinking that by then it was already too late to do very much. If the President had possessed the boundless energy of the New Deal years or even of the early years of the war, he might have managed to reverse the huge historical processes which had already been set in motion. But he did not have that sort of energy any longer, and he could not have regained it even if he had lived longer.

Even in the summer of 1944, he had already begun to do things most uncharacteristic of his best years. The truth is that, despite the Quebec and Yalta conferences and the national election of 1944, the last year and a half of the President's life was a time when his superb machine of life was slowly but inexorably running down, because of the long and taxing use he had made of it. As early as the spring of 1944, the intermittent low fever he had that winter drove him to spend close to a month at Bernard M. Baruch's place in South Carolina, Hobcaw Barony. Mrs. Rutherfurd drove over for lunch with the President at Hobcaw from Aiken; but there were almost no regular guests at Hobcaw except the essential members of the President's staff and people who came down on business. The enormous mechanisms of a world war were already in place, all around the world. Everywhere they were moving forward inexorably towards their planned goals. Even by the time Roosevelt went to Hobcaw, the major decisions had been taken. Yet the strain was unremitting, and it was at last beginning to exact a heavy price.

So much is clear, yet it seems doubtful whether the rights and wrongs of the 1944 campaign will ever be sorted out. Three points only are quite certain. First, the President's vitality was already heavily depleted by the first months of 1944. Second, there is not a shred of evidence that the President had already suffered light strokes or any of the other really serious impairments that have sometimes been rumored. Third, it is none the less wrong for any man to be a candidate for the Presidency, whether for a first term or reelection, if he is not reasonably confident his health will hold up under the burdens of the office. Where the uncertainty lies is in the right way to balance the three certainties here listed.

At a guess, two factors decided Roosevelt to run again.

On the one hand, he had no fear of death, partly because of his religious faith. He truly believed that when his time had come, he would then hear the summons that all hear in the end—but not before. On the other hand, he also believed that any politically imaginable successor would be wholly unable to master the ramified complexities of war all around the world, or the comparable complexities which could be expected from the later task of worldwide peacemaking. Hence he was determined to finish the job, as he put it.

Luckily, he had long since faced the fact that Henry A. Wallace, when too far removed from agrarian realities, was really a great goose in human form. Just as fortunately, he therefore acquiesced in the choice of Harry S Truman to replace Wallace as the Vice-Presidential candidate, partly because this choice was good politics, but also because he had much respect for Truman's work in the Senate. As for the political campaign, the fate of the Republican candidate, Thomas E. Dewey, was all but sealed when the President made his famous "Fala" speech, solemnly defending his small, cross-tempered Scotch terrier against alleged Republican slanders. It was the craftiest political put-down one American Presidential candidate has ever inflicted on another; and after the Fala speech, poor Dewey was reduced to fruitless flailing against an opponent wholly beyond his reach. Yet even so, Roosevelt, the instinctive campaigner, gave almost a day to touring the New York City boroughs just before the election through incessant gusts of rain and in bone-chilling raw cold.

The President's last Christmas followed his election to a fourth term, and then came Yalta. Normally, the President would have been enormously picked up by a long sea voyage across the Atlantic and as far as Malta, before the air journey to the Crimea. Instead, those who had not seen Roosevelt for some time were much alarmed by his appearance at Yalta. Hopkins was there, too, for after the Quebec meeting the President had evidently concluded he could not do without the partnership which had been so close before Hopkins's move out of the White House. Yet Hopkins was not well enough to go to the meetings at Yalta, and he spent most of his time in his bedroom, where the leading Americans and most of the leading British at the conference went frequently to consult him.

Even so, when the President was finally on his way home, Hopkins was still so unwell that he had to leave the party and go to Marrakech for a rest in the sunshine. Just as sad for the President, too, was the death of his close friend and unfailingly shrewd military aide, General Edwin "Pa" Watson, who suffered a fatal stroke on the way home through the Mediterranean. By the time Roosevelt reached Washington, in short, the dusk of life was already thickening around him.

Luckily for him and for the United States, his wartime job was nearly done by then. On 6 June 1944, D-Day had come in Europe, and he had read the D-Day prayer to the nation. The prayer was all but completely answered by early 1945, for the German war machine, once so awe-inspiring, was shattered long before Adolf Hitler began his last lunatic attempts to organize a national *Götterdämmerung*. As early as the journey back from Yalta, too, the President's ship received the first flash from Admiral Nimitz announcing U.S. attacks on military targets in the Japanese islands. The long drive northwards by General MacArthur and Admiral Nimitz could hardly fail to reach its objective pretty soon. The San Francisco Conference to found the United Nations was also due to open before long, and the President was determined to be there and to deliver the opening speech.

Yet the now-shrinking number of those who had access to the President must all have known what was coming soon. Robert Sherwood saw him to report on a visit to General MacArthur's headquarters in the Pacific, and he immediately concluded that Roosevelt was a desperately ill man. General Albert C. Wedemeyer, who had replaced Stilwell, went home for consultation in early 1945, and as he was now a theater commander he was received briefly just before he went back to China.

I still recall the cold chill that fell over the staff meeting Wedemeyer held on his return to Kunming. After he had run through the necessary business with his staff and the air staff, the General paused as though in doubt about whether to continue, and then did so with quiet solemnity. He had had "the honor to see our President," as he phrased it, and he believed he was the last official visitor before the President went for a rest at Warm Springs. Here he paused again, but went on. "I think I should tell you all confidentially, our President is now so unwell that I fear he may be lost to us soon." Most could not believe Wedemeyer, although he was a careful observer; for Roosevelt had led the nation so long that the United States without Roosevelt could hardly be imagined. I heard one or two who thought Wedemeyer likely to be right draw in their breaths sharply; and so we all filed out.

On 12 April the President was sitting cheerfully in his living room at Warm Springs, chatting with Mrs. Rutherfurd while her friend Mme. Shoumatoff worked on a portrait of him. Quite suddenly, he suffered a heavy cerebral hemorrhage. He said only, "I have a terrific headache," and fell back unconscious. Mrs. Rutherfurd took him in her arms, but she soon saw there was no hope, and so she left for Aiken at once. Miss Laura Delano meanwhile telephoned Mrs. Roosevelt in Washington, at first to tell her only that the President had "fainted" and had been put to bed. But soon enough the real news came through, and before long the whole world was told. Like everyone else who was then more than a child, I remember precisely how the news of the President's death reached Kunming, and how not a few young men in uniform in the 14th Air Force could be seen quite openly sobbing for this loss which made uncounted Americans feel as though a father had been taken from them.

Americans have a way of showing their feelings when they lose leaders they have relied upon and held in affection, so the crowds on the station platforms waited through the night for the sad train carrying the dead President from Warm Springs to Washington, and even greater crowds stood for hours to salute the train carrying him on his final journey from Washington to Hyde Park. There, in the rose garden, the other American war leaders, mostly men of his choosing, came to hear the short and ancient burial service. And on three sides of the rose garden, lines of soldiers, sailors, and marines in uniform wore the ribbons commemorating the grim siege of Cassino, the fighting in Solomons Slot, the cruel battles of the first North African campaign, the fights at Leyte, Medjez El Bab, and Midway, the costly enterprise against Ploesti, the hard flying over the Hump to China, and the bitter hand-to-hand contest for Iwo Jima.

It only remains to describe the virtues which made Roosevelt a great war President—for his few errors have already been touched upon. The outcome is enough to testify to the greatness of these virtues. By any standard, the President's successes reduce his occasional errors to insignificance. He did not seek to interfere in the detailed command

155

decisions of the armed services, as Winston Churchill did continuously. But he still required to be continuously informed in much detail, and he still kept all the major threads in his own hands, straightening out a kink or tangle whenever one appeared. He chose the men who helped lead the war with altogether remarkable good judgment too. It is to be doubted, in truth, whether the American government ever boasted before, or will boast again, such a constellation of great American public servants and military leaders as Washington contained in the Second World War.

For an entire generation after the war ended, President Roosevelt's successors in the White House regularly turned to the Roosevelt veterans for wise counsel when the going got rough. With one of them, Robert A. Lovett, President Kennedy even went so far as to offer a choice of the Secretaryships of State, Defense, and the Treasury. The great officials whom Roosevelt had recruited in the war emergency further made much of the glory of the not inglorious administration of President Truman, and today I wonder sadly whether we shall ever see their like again. Sadly, I wonder too whether we shall ever see another leader of the U.S. Army with the all-around greatness of George C. Marshall, or an Air Force leader with the tough, concentrated intelligence and crafty courage of H. H. Arnold, or a Chief of Naval Operations to compare in fighting spirit and general astuteness with the grim, relentless Ernest King.

Maybe I have become a sorry praiser of the past, as men over seventy tend to do; but this is a personal memoir, and if I truly feel there were giants in the land in the Roosevelt years, I claim the right to say so. Even so, I have not yet come to what seems to me the greatest of Franklin Roosevelt's contributions as a war President. The nature of that contribution is best conveyed, I believe, by an experience of my own; and another right I claim in this memoir is to indicate how I came to form the judgments of Roosevelt herein set down.

As I explained earlier, I reached Hong Kong on Pearl Harbor Day with the Japanese forces already across the city's frontier on the mainland. I had few Hong Kong friends, but one of them luckily was Emily Hahn, then of *The New Yorker*. She arranged to put me up in someone's apartment on the mid-level of the mountain up which the island part of the city climbs toward the lofty Peak. The President went before Congress to ask for a declaration of war the day after Pearl Harbor, and in order to hear him I waited in the otherwise empty mid-level apartment where there was an antiquated although once-costly radio. I was already worried, too, for I felt personally guilty to be trapped in Hong Kong, with no possible chance of being able to rejoin my unit, the AVG, despite Chennault's orders. The President's speech to the Joint Session was heard in Hong Kong, whether directly or by rebroadcast I have never figured out, when the dusk had already passed. The apartment was very imperfectly blacked out, so no lights could be lit and I was in perfect darkness. By then, the Japanese were rather heavily bombing the mid-level, and the bombs were falling only blocks away. The radio was also so faulty that I had to lie on the floor with my head just under it, in order to hear much of anything. I got the President's drift, which was easy enough to predict in any case, but I caught no more than one word in two—hardly more than enough to be reminded of the timbre of his voice.

Yet in these fairly gloomy and frustrating circumstances, it never for one moment occurred to me that there might be the smallest doubt about the outcome of the vast war the President was asking the Congress to declare in proper form. Nor did I find any other American throughout the entire war who ever doubted the eventual outcome. Even more than the feeling that there were giants in the land, I now feel nostalgia for the absolute confidence in the American future which was the necessary foundation of this total absence of doubt. Hope was in fact Franklin Roosevelt's greatest gift to his fellow Americans. Partly he gave us hope by his deeds, when he came to office in a time that seemed utterly devoid of hope. But even more, he gave us hope because all could see that he himself felt not the slightest doubt about the future at any time in his years as President. Defeats there might be (though they were rare) on this bill or that in Congress. Fearful military misfortunes there were, with Pearl Harbor itself the most notable and hard to comprehend. Grounds for even a slight temporary loss of hope there never were, however—at any rate in the President's mind; and somehow, his mind formed the minds of the overwhelming majority of other Americans who watched him in action in those years of hope.

Acknowledgments and Credits

The task of compiling the picture sections of this book was enormously facilitated by the staff of the Franklin D. Roosevelt Library at Hyde Park, N.Y. Our thanks go to its director, William Emerson, and its photo archivist, Paul McLaughlin, as well as to their assistants for help and patience far beyond the call of duty. All photographs not specifically credited below come from the Franklin D. Roosevelt Library's unique archive of photographs, and are herewith gratefully acknowledged.

Special thanks go also to Margaret Suckley, the President's cousin, for permission to reproduce snapshots #79 and #89.

PHOTOGRAPHS AND CARTOONS:
Fox Photos: 87
Historical Pictures Service: 68
Tom McAvoy/Life: 75, 76
National Foundation for Infantile Paralysis: 36
New York Daily News: 64
United Press International: 34, 42, 45, 46, 47, 49, 50, 51, 59, 60, 63, 65, 74, 83, 84, 91
Wide World Photos: 30, 39, 43, 44, 57, 61, 71, 90
Library of Congress (Clifford Berryman): 58